PURE STYLE

OUTSIDE

PURE STYLE
OUTSIDE

JANE CUMBERBATCH

PHOTOGRAPHY BY
PIA TRYDE

RYLAND
PETERS
& SMALL

Creative Director **Jacqui Small**

Editorial Director **Anne Ryland**

Art Editor **Penny Stock**

Editor **Zia Mattocks**

Production **Kate Mackillop**

Stylist **Jane Cumberbatch**

Assistant Stylist **Fiona Craig-McFeely**

Assistant Stylist **Alice Douglas**

First Published in Great Britain in 1998
by Ryland Peters & Small
Cavendish House, 51–5 Mortimer Street,
London W1N 7TD

Text copyright © 1998 Jane Cumberbatch
Design and photographs copyright
© 1998 Ryland Peters & Small

Printed and bound in Hong Kong
by Toppan Printing Co.

ISBN: 1 900518 49 X

A CIP catalogue record for this book is available from
the British Library.

Contents

PURE STYLE OUTSIDE: NEW IDEAS FOR
SIMPLE, STYLISH OUTDOOR LIVING.

INTRODUCTION

Pure Style Outside is not a gardening book
packed with daunting Latin names, impossible
planting schemes, trendy plant varieties and
grand ideas for garden furniture. It is about
making the best of your outside space – however
small – whether it is a balcony, a vegetable patch
or a back yard. *Pure Style Outside* is about being
practical, using functional but pleasing tools in a
stylish, simple way, and looking at resourceful
solutions for making your outside area as
colourful, textural, sensuous, and as pleasing to
be in as any room inside your home.

Pure Style Outside is about colour: the shades that appear in nature, such as sky blues, rose pinks, sunflower yellows and cabbage greens, and the decorative ideas which will work well with these natural elements, like soft white cotton canvas, trellis painted minty green or terracotta coloured walls. It looks at the surfaces and textures – both natural and artificial – that work together to make the out-side a living, organic space, such as blistered, peeling paintwork on doors and walls; old rusting metal furniture and shiny clean tools; earthy, weathered flowerpots and mossy, worn red-brick paving stones. *Pure Style Outside* is about being practical and adopting vernacular styles for everything from fencing to garden tools. There are loads of ideas for planting rows of vibrant dahlias, climbing roses, clematis and morning glory, towering foxgloves and delphiniums; pots or beds of basil, rosemary, thyme and mint; and other edible produce like tomatoes, courgettes, beans and lettuces. Most plants are quite ordinary, yet they are either beautiful to look at or delicious to eat; and they are all possible to grow from readily available seeds, tubers or young plants.

PURE STYLE OUTSIDE IS

also about experiencing the obvious, simple pleasures in life (the very elements that many of us neglect in the hurly-burly of daily living) like eating home-grown herbs or tomatoes, cutting your own roses for the table, or the sheer peace of sitting outside on a warm starry night. It looks at being self-sufficient, with ideas for creating a utilitarian garden for growing your own healthy produce – an increasing trend among people who are tired of consuming tasteless vacuum-packed fruit and vegetables from supermarkets. *Pure Style Outside* focuses on the decorative aspects of open-air living and the elements required to make your outside area more like a room, and it is full of inspiring ideas for good-value durable fabrics, simple garden furniture and accessories, and basic but good-looking tableware. It is also about eating, with suggestions for delicious outdoor food, using plain good-quality ingredients, from pasta with home-made tomato sauce, to grilled vegetables and delicious treats for tea. Lastly, *Pure Style Outside* shows you how to appreciate the sensuous qualities of the natural elements that make an outside space a living, breathing place – water, light and shade, scent and texture – whether it is the cool, refreshing atmosphere of a wet garden after rain or the feel of soft, lush grass underfoot.

ELEMEN

TS

Bring life to your outside space with organic textures and colour. Take a simple but practical approach and invest in basic old-fashioned tools that do the job properly. Take inspiration from vernacular styles for decorative and functional detailing. Choose colourful flowers that are easy to grow, and use fabrics and furniture to make your outside area a luxurious place.

Colour

Colours change endlessly according to the seasons, the weather and the time of day. Strong sunlight on white walls dazzles the eyes with a harshness that makes us reach for a pair of sunglasses, whereas a dull day actually intensifies colours so they appear to leap out of the greyness. Consider colour in every aspect of outside living: plants, architectural details, furniture, fabrics and food. There is beauty in the simplest elements: a climbing white rose; green peas and beans growing in a vegetable patch; and a shady table laid with a crisp white cloth and bowls of green salad. Simple colour schemes for plants look distinctive, such as rows of brilliant-yellow sunflowers; a white wall covered with tumbling tendrils of sky-blue morning glory; or a window box painted pale green and planted with hedges of dwarf lavender. Enhance a sense of greenery by painting doors and windows in garden greens. Take note of vernacular styles, such as the colours of blinds and shutters in Mediterranean villages, or the shades of green paint that decorate sheds and fences in old-fashioned allotments. Make your outside space more of a room with colourful cushions and awnings: try classic shades of white or blue, or bold combinations like vivid orange and pink.

White

The simplicity of white makes it a purist's dream colour and a versatile tool: white flowers can be used as a foil for greenery and white garden accessories look crisp. Although I am tempted to grow flowers in all my favourite colours, I stick to mainly white as ultimately it is the look most soothing to the urban eye. Each spring I look forward to the sweet-smelling white flowers that bloom on the climbing *Rosa* 'Madame Alfred Carrière', an old-fashioned rose that thrives in its shady environment. White *Clematis montana* produces hundreds of star-like flowers that spread in May along the railings of my roof terrace. Perfect for shady spots is the less-rampant *C.* 'Henryi', which produces huge white flowers during the summer and has even bloomed in a warm December.

Whitewash

Stone

Canvas

Pebble

Spiky foxgloves are good for height and attract bees, but most are biennial. For smart, almost instant window-box material I buy pots of white asters, available from nurseries at the beginning of summer. Bright whitewashed walls are the vernacular style on sundrenched Mediterranean patios and the look is easy to create with white exterior paint. I use white emulsion to transform everything from flowerpots to trellis; when it looks grubby or worn I simply repaint it, although old chairs and tables with blistered, peeling paint can look charming. Hardly practical, but white cushions and cloths look wonderful outside and create an airy, summery feel. I use old sheets for tablecloths and prewashed canvas for cushions and awnings, so at least the whole lot can be revived in the wash.

Blue

Blue, the colour of the sea and sky, and flowers like blue-bells, agapanthus and delphiniums, combines well with pink, white or yellow. As a single colour it looks dramatic: a wall covered with jewel-like morning glory blooms, a fence bordered with cornflowers, or a bank of papery irises. Sheds and window boxes look jaunty painted in the bright, breezy shades seen in all seaside towns. Look to Aegean villages for inspiration and create a rich sea blue for tubs and flowerpots by mixing a few drops of blue universal stainer into a can of white emulsion. A white-washed patio looks fabulous with blue and white cotton cushions and tablecloths, while practical, inexpensive bright-blue plastic cloths and plates look cheery outside.

Cloud

Bluebell

Sea

Berry

Green

The array of greens in a vegetable patch illustrates the vast spectrum of shades: purplish green cabbages, lime-green lettuces and glossy peas packed in their pods. However commonplace, there is beauty in silvery green lavender, shiny rosemary, lime-green alchemilla and even a stretch of lush lawn. In spring, young leaves are luminous and bright with a yellow hue, and as the season progresses they darken to richer shades of green. Potting-shed greens, which blend unobtrusively with their surroundings, are the

Bean

Fig

Mint

Shed

shades devised by generations of gardeners who have painted fences, sheds, doors and seats in basic colours from ironmongers. Even if foliage is sparse, you can create an illusion of greenery by painting a bench, table, chair or door in anything from rich olive to paler leafy tones. Sea green or mint are more modern and have a Mediterranean feel; they are shades that look smart against galvanized metal buckets and pink and lavender-coloured flowers. Green-and-white striped canvas is useful for deck chairs and awnings, and is the sort of utilitarian material that is still found in traditional ironmongers.

Pink

Pink is a classic garden colour, and photographs of glorious pink and lavender borders of delphiniums, foxgloves, roses, sweet peas and peonies are what we hanker after and pour over in glossy garden books – the images would be complete with ourselves in appropriate gardening attire (a big floppy straw sun hat, with secateurs and an old trug). Nature has so exquisitely matched pink with green: think of spiky lavender heads on trim silvery green stems, or fuchsia-pink foxglove bells on lime-green stalks. I love to see trellis with pink rambling roses, or a garden wall flanked by towering pink hollyhocks. Fluffy purplish allium balls are good for creating

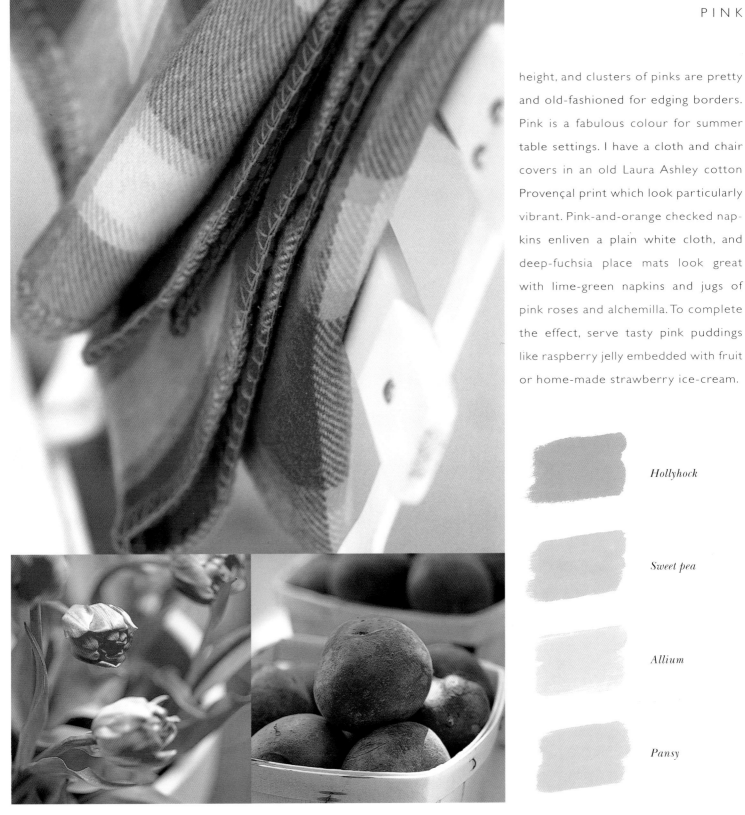

height, and clusters of pinks are pretty and old-fashioned for edging borders. Pink is a fabulous colour for summer table settings. I have a cloth and chair covers in an old Laura Ashley cotton Provençal print which look particularly vibrant. Pink-and-orange checked napkins enliven a plain white cloth, and deep-fuchsia place mats look great with lime-green napkins and jugs of pink roses and alchemilla. To complete the effect, serve tasty pink puddings like raspberry jelly embedded with fruit or home-made strawberry ice-cream.

Hollyhock

Sweet pea

Allium

Pansy

Orange

Earth

Tomato

Pumpkin

Flowerpot

vegetable garden look pleasing and deter caterpillars and snails, and pots of tall orange lilies look good on a balcony or terrace. Orange and pink are an exciting combination – try modern hybrid orange roses with old-fashioned pinks and cerises, and there are rich orange and pink varieties in the dahlia family, until recently considered rather kitsch. Dahlias are beautiful, but need

Garish and regimented municipal-park displays have made orange flowers unpopular with sensitive gardeners, and although splashes of orange would be unwelcome in a classic pink, lavender and white country-garden border, it is a wonderful, daring hot colour that can add vibrancy and life to an outside space. Borders of marigolds in a

flavour and decoration. There is something inviting and luxuriant about the neat avenues of trees laden with jewel-like oranges in southern Europe. A bowl of fat oranges with their leaves still attached makes a wonderful table decoration, and white jugs stuffed with marigolds also create vibrant splashes of colour on a white tablecloth.

to be grown in an orderly fashion, say, as part of a vegetable plot, and the cut flowers look wonderful in a simple jam jar. I vowed not to have any orange in my almost-white garden, but couldn't resist packs of nasturtium seeds. They are foolproof to plant in pots and trail up a wigwam of sticks producing endless orange, yellow and scarlet flowers, which can be added to salads for nutty

Yellow

Candle

Honeysuckle

Nasturtium

Hay

Reassuring bursts of yellow daffodils, narcissi and tulips punctuate city gardens and the countryside in spring, confirming that all the colour hasn't drained away during the winter. I like to plant pots and window boxes outside the kitchen with dwarf daffodils and narcissi, which have a wonderful heady scent. As a child I used to plant daffodil bulbs and keep them in a cupboard until spring; it was sheer magic to watch the shoots grow and produce a mass of yellow trumpets. I also have a fascination for sunflowers and cannot believe they can grow quite so tall and produce such giant glowing heads in so few weeks. Try planting rows of sunflowers to make a natural border or to create shelter from the wind. Other yellow favourites include honeysuckle, which is easy to grow from cuttings and has a scent that intensifies during the evening, and pale hollyhocks flanking a front door. For the outside table, yellow and green make a stylish combination. Grill courgettes and decorate them with edible courgette flowers – wildly expensive in smart greengrocers but virtually free if you grow your own. For pudding, I serve creamy yellow peaches in simple butter-yellow pottery bowls.

Surfaces

Organic, natural and synthetic surfaces combine to make the garden a living, breathing space. Nature creates an ever-changing textural picture: consider dry, sun-baked terracotta and the same surface after a heavy storm, darkened and glistening with puddles. Many surfaces improve with age and exposure to the elements, such as sun-blistered peeling paint on an old garden table, the bleached silvery grey of a weathered oak chair, or an irregular hand-thrown terracotta pot, crumbling with moss and age. For boundaries there are diverse materials such as old red brickwork, New England-style featherboarding, and simple wood-and-wire or stick fencing. For underfoot, old red-brick pavers can be laid in a herringbone pattern to edge borders or make practical pathways in a vegetable plot. Smooth square terracotta tiles look distinctive laid in a regular checquerboard pattern, and a line of old worn York flagstones creates a simple, useful path. Alternatively, there are cobbles, gravel and luxurious

soft lawn. Water is a sensuous, cooling surface, and merely filling up an old sink or bucket lined with pebbles and shells creates a simple makeshift pool. Textural fabrics for outdoor use include cotton canvas for awnings and woven cane or rattan for seating.

Texture

Contrasting textures in the garden are surprising and exciting, with tactile elements like rough weatherboarding, blistering paint, balls of hairy string — useful for a multitude of gardening jobs — and besom brooms with twiggy bristles. The feel of a rough weathered flowerpot or a bleached wooden trug together with the smooth coolness of metal tools make any garden task a sensuous experience. After pounding city streets, treat tired feet to a soft and springy lawn, or a carpet of heady

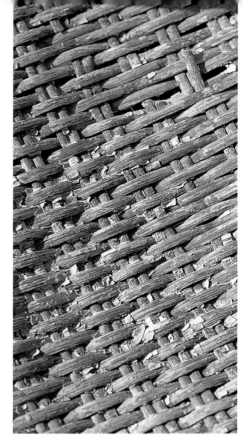

scented thyme or camomile. It is satisfying to march down a crunchy gravel path or sunbathe on worn, lichen-encrusted York flagstones, while teak decking, a good material for a poolside area or terrace, feels smooth to the touch. No-nonsense coarse canvas is a natural, practical fabric for seat covers and awnings, and acts as a foil to indulgent feather-filled cushions and soft throws for luxurious siestas. There are also the textures of a dry garden, which contrast with those of damp soil and dripping plants, newly watered or after a storm, when leaves are bent double by jewel-like drops of water.

Deciding what lies underfoot in your garden space is important in both practical and visual terms. The courtyard at the back of my house is laid with old brick pavers that were found ten years ago in a Cambridgeshire salvage yard. They are a rich red terracotta, which has weathered enough to look as if they were laid when the house was built nearly 300 years ago.

Underfoot

the eye in exciting and sometimes unexpected directions. A diminutive flower and vegetable garden that I know in America's Catskill Mountains is criss-crossed by a series of swept hard-earth pathways, an idea transplanted from the southern states where the owner grew up. An enclosed herb and vegetable garden in Connecticut

A weekly sweep with a stiff-bristled broom is enough to keep the area pristine, and after very wet spells I hose it down with a mild bleach solution to keep slippery moss at bay. Old creamy yellow York flagstones were another option that I considered, but they were more costly to transport and to lay per square metre. Garden paths create a sense of order and lead

the cool of the evening. They can be obtained quite cheaply from builder's merchants in France, Spain and Italy, or from local suppliers who import them. If you have time, it is also worth looking out for tiles salvaged from old farmhouses. The irregularity of rough, uneven cobbled surfaces is appealing, and I am inspired by the decorative marble-chip patios, pavements and

is more formally bisected by uneven brick avenues, while a London allotment belonging to a friend of mine is divided by irregularly shaped slabs of stone. Smooth terracotta tiles laid in simple geometric checquerboard patterns are perfect for hot Mediterranean patios as they retain heat and are delicious to walk on barefoot in

at the beach and is a useful surface for roof gardens or small terraces where heavier materials are not suitable. For a greener, softer garden surface, the obvious choice is a velvety lawn. More unusual are flagstones with herbs like camomile or thyme planted between the cracks, which emanate a delicious scent when crushed underfoot.

alleyways found in many Spanish villages. Other aggregates, such as gravel, create textural, crunchy paths that are practical and reasonably maintenance-free. Specialized suppliers will provide everything from white marble cobblestones and green marble pebbles, to beach pebbles, cockleshells and terracotta shingle. Teak or pine decking has a seaside look inspired by boardwalks

Boundaries

The earliest gardens were contained for practical reasons – for privacy, to exclude vermin and simply to enclose a cultivated area of ground. As well as protecting plants from frost, gardens surrounded by walls of red brick feel secretive and romantic. Visit old walled gardens in grounds of historic houses, such as Holkham Hall in Norfolk, which are a great source of inspiration. Also, gather ideas from vernacular styles for fences and walls when choosing a boundary for your garden or vegetable patch: New England linear picket fencing is charming and can be found in garden centres on both sides of the Atlantic, and flat plank fencing, seen worldwide, can be painted white, garden green, or left unfinished to weather and bleach. Improvised fences of sticks or pieces of curved wattle look rustic and decorative in small vegetable gardens, while a row of espaliered fruit trees or pleached limes and neatly clipped box hedges create natural, green boundaries. To create decorative borders for beds, try rows of smooth, round pebbles, lengths of bent or woven wattle, or scalloped Victorian terracotta tiles.

Another boundary that should not be overlooked is the facade of the house. Even if the only outside space you have is a window box, think about the colour and texture of the wall around it. A white-painted box planted with white daisies and set against white featherboarding evokes a simple New England cottage, while whitewashed

walls create a Mediterranean feel and are ideal for small patios as they reflect light and enhance the sense of space. Climbing roses and honeysuckle look pretty trained up the facade of a brick house. Alternatively, the flat features of modern precast brick walling can be alleviated with paint. The rich barn red that wooden cabins and sheds are painted all over North America and Scandinavia makes a strong backdrop for plants and garden furniture. I mixed up a greenish blue shade for a stretch of new wall, and this also makes a perfect ground for plants or topiary box trees in metal buckets.

Utilitarian gardener

Efficient gardeners are methodical and rigorous about their duties. They rely on good, basic tools and, above all, have a passion for growing things. Sheds, lean-tos and other covered areas are utilitarian spaces in which to store all their garden paraphernalia, whether it is a supply of firewood or an array of pots and garden tools. Resourceful individuals cobble together sheets of corrugated metal, salvaged wood and doors to create makeshift shelters. Then there are glass greenhouses for nurturing delicate seedlings, overwintering cuttings and growing frost-intolerant fruits and vegetables. The British are very fond of sheds, which lurk at the bottom of many suburban gardens and are stuffed with everything from Wellington boots, pea sticks, seed trays and tools, to old-fashioned insecticide pumps. Another essential is a compost bin, filled with grass cuttings, leaves and other potential mulch. Even a city dweller with little outside space can reserve a corner for organizing gardening gear. Make sure the area is watertight and perhaps construct a lean-to shelter. Paint wooden crates for storing pots, use a side table as a potting bench, build shelves for tools, or screw in hooks for string and raffia. A window-box gardener might find that a canvas bag does the job.

Potting shed

On a train journey to any large English city you see patchworks of allotment gardens, the plots often sandwiched between bus depots and electricity pylons. The allotment holders are a mixture of knowledgeable old-timers, who remember the self-sufficiency practised by everyone during the Second World War, and a younger generation of gardeners who want their children to know that vegetables come from the earth, rather than from Cellophane packs. Everyone has a shed, no matter how makeshift or eccentric, and a look inside any might reveal deck chairs; old plastic bottles to up-end on sticks to make improvised scarecrows; string; raffia; yoghurt pots for seedlings; and an array of tools. Vegetable patches and allotment-style gardens need year-round attention, from spring when bulbs begin flowering and the soil is hoed and fertilized in preparation for planting, through summer when fruits and vegetables ripen, weeds are battled with and watering is a constant activity, to autumn when plants are cut back and produce is harvested. These gardens require soil that is fertile, well drained, well tilled and weed free. Light and crumbly soil allows air to enter which sustains the organisms that make up healthy earth, so if soil is hard when dry, and sticky when wet, dig in as much organic material as you can to lighten it. Inexpensive meters for testing the acidity of soil are available – a pH of 6.5 is ideal for general purposes. With increased popularity in organic growing methods and less reliance on chemical pesticides and fertilizers, many gardeners are keen to make their own compost and grow plants such as marigolds, which are said to destroy snails and caterpillars. Yet it is rather impractical not to resort to manufactured fertilizers if you have restricted growing space. I buy bone meal and apply a weekly dose of Miracle Grow to help my roses, del-phiniums, foxgloves, clematis, herbs, lettuces and tomatoes. I also collect bags of well-rotted horse manure from a nearby city farm, which I apply in copious quantities in early summer and autumn. If you have space, a com-post heap is essential, with ingredients such as tea bags, eggshells, vegetable and fruit peelings, manure and grass cuttings. Keep it moist with water and turn the heap occasionally to aerate it.

Structures

There is a fashion for growing anything from nasturtiums and tomatoes to runner beans and sweet peas up wigwam shapes made of canes or twigs. The effect, inspired by old-fashioned bean setts, is easy to achieve, decorative, and a practical way of training plants. Single sticks of wood set in serried rows are another functional but charming way of training beans and other climbers that do not produce heavy fruits, and 'hedges' of thin twiggy sticks are great for training sweet peas. For really simple but effective structures, buy lengths of chicken wire from hardware shops. Alternatively, simple wooden square trellis, available from any good garden centre, looks really smart painted a shade of garden green: I used it for training clematis over a rather ugly stretch of brick wall on my roof garden. Arbours, arches and pergolas create shady areas in which to relax, and are also decorative ways of supporting climbing roses and other brilliant blooms. Simple metal rose arches can be obtained from garden centres or mail-order catalogues, and the rather unsightly finish that many come in can be concealed with tough enamel paint. Twiggy pergolas made of sticks are particularly romantic and easy to construct, but coat the ends that sit in the earth with an antirot preparation. A shady vine pergola is like a little outside room, and can be made by training a grapevine or another vigorous climber over a wooden or wire-and-metal structure.

Tools

Wooden-handled garden shears for trimming hedges and cutting back shrubs.

A set of all-metal trowel, dibber and fork – essential tools for potting plants and seedlings – are practical and easy to clean.

Keep a besom broom for sweeping up leaves and twigs, and a supply of cane pea sticks to build wigwams to train climbing plants.

I have a few totally indispensable tools for my gardening activities, which live in the old coal cellar – my version of a potting shed. Most of my gardening is carried out in pots and window boxes, and my watering can is used twice a day in hot weather to satisfy the thirst of the potted plants. The essential fork, trowel and dibber are normally kept tucked into a pot, and secateurs and a

A sturdy trowel is probably the most essential tool for a city gardener to plant window boxes and pots.

This plastic apron is practical gardening attire, together with a pair of tough gloves like these vinyl-coated ones.

Curvy and compact, traditional wooden trugs are shaped perfectly for carrying tools, plants and other gardening kit.

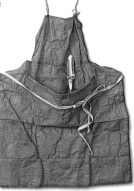

Bright-green refuse sacks are a jollier alternative to the ubiquitous black bin bags.

A big plastic holdall like this is inexpensive and can be used to carry everything from picnic gear to logs from the wood shed.

I have several metal watering cans and this galvanized example is good because its boxy proportions make it easy to carry and pour.

pair of tough gloves are always at hand for pruning. There are also canes, wire and pieces of string for training new growth, and hats, old shirts and gum boots. I also keep cans of emulsion for painting trellis, pots and furniture, and plastic bottles of diluted washing-up liquid to rid the roses of greenfly and more potent insecticide to deal with blackfly that plague the nasturtiums.

A rake for leaves, a traditional pitchfork and a solid spade with a wooden handle are all useful implements for the gardener.

Raffia and string are invaluable for all sorts of jobs, from tying tomato plants to canes, to hanging up bundles of bulbs to dry.

Plant labels need not be boring to look at. Metal or wooden garden tags are much more stylish than plastic ones – and they are not expensive.

Gumboots are the most sensible footwear for gardening jobs on soggy wet days – this pair is lined with leather for extra warmth.

Containers

Almost anything will do as a plant container: plastic bowls, old sinks, terracotta pots, wooden tubs and galvanized metal buckets are just some examples. Containers make focal points within a garden and can be moved whenever you feel like it. Try a pair of tubs with standard box or bay trees on either side of a door, or mass together terracotta pots filled with herbs. Create a miniature garden on a windowsill or balcony with window boxes containing anything from little lavender hedges to trailing nasturtiums, vegetables or herbs. Wooden seed trays, picket-fence window boxes and twiggy troughs are all useful for displaying pots of herbs, spring bulbs and summer bedding plants. For added colour I paint pots in shades of green, blue or white. Good drainage is the key to success, and normal-size pots with a central hole need only a few stones in the bottom before being filled with soil. For a well-balanced potting medium, use soil that is light, friable, easily drained and nourishing. Mix heavy soil

with sharp river sand, and light soil with rich loam. Add granulated peat to help retain moisture, and fertilizer to provide nourishment. With the addition of compost and regular feeding, potted plants will remain healthy in the same soil for many years.

Terracotta

Shapes range from traditional potting-shed flowerpots to giant Ali-Baba urns. Good garden specialists import wonderful textural terracotta pots from Spain, Italy, France and Morocco. Salvage and reclamation yards are good sources of old hand-thrown flowerpots – I have four or five beautiful worn examples that came from the glasshouses of a big old country mansion. Machine-made terracotta pots look uniform and lack the texture and irregularities of hand-thrown examples. To add instant character to cheap pots from garden centres I mix up a wash of white emulsion coloured with green, blue or terracotta. Pots left out in the elements weather quite quickly, but you can accelerate the process by smearing them with yoghurt to encourage green moss to grow. I use giant terracotta pots in all shapes for planting clematis, trailing tomatoes, honeysuckle and lavender, and rectangular containers placed against a wall for growing taller things like foxgloves and delphiniums. Create a windowsill or balcony kitchen garden with herbs planted in individual pots: rosemary, parsley, mint, marjoram, rocket, sage,

Ideal for a rooftop or balcony vegetable garden is a long tom flowerpot painted in vibrant lime-green emulsion with a wigwam of pea sticks and raffia to support a cherry tomato plant.

A pot painted with lime-green emulsion and planted with an ornamental kale cabbage looks good on a windowsill or arranged in a row with three or four others along a terrace wall.

Old terracotta bowls look decorative planted with herbs or bedding plants like pansies, but make sure there is a hole for drainage.

A shallow terracotta planter looks good filled with several low-growing plants such as mind-your-own-business.

A 19th-century-style terracotta rhubarb forcer with a removable lid can either be planted with tiny trailing flowers or left empty as a decorative feature.

thyme and basil (provided it is sunny, warm and sheltered) grow well with a strict daily watering regime. Or use terracotta pots for vegetables: I have attempted lettuces, trailing tomatoes and dwarf cherry tomatoes with success. For a structured look, round box balls look architectural in square terracotta pots, while little box or bay standards suit pots with a round shape.

left to right

Pansies planted in a wall pot painted with a wash of white and terracotta emulsion for a weathered effect; two terracotta tom pots planted with an amaryllis and a topiary box tree.

Ornamental curly kale cabbages in a simple
galvanized metal container make an unusual
decoration for the table or windowsill.

An old powder-blue enamelled camping dish
is an idea for planting violas and other
tiny flowering plants.

A basic metal tin is ideal for growing wheat
grass – the latest organic wonder root, which
can be liquidized to make a nourishing drink.

The silvery green leaves and rough texture
of aromatic lavender work well with metal
containers like this florist's display bucket.

A weathered metal bucket is a no-nonsense,
yet pleasing, container for a box standard.

A shapely bay standard in a metal bucket can
be placed on a table to create a sense of height.

Metal

Functional and simple metal kit for the garden, such as galvanized metal watering cans and dustbins, and corrugated-iron shacks and sheds have a rough, honest appeal and create a foil to the softness of plants and flowers. Metal plant containers – whether they are buckets, troughs, bowls or old cans – have a tough, utilitarian feel, and their modern look makes a refreshing change from traditional stone or terracotta containers. The silvery grey colour of the metal works well with greenery, and the textured galvanized surfaces look good contrasted with silvery grey-green lavender leaves or shiny dark-green rosemary bushes. Simple architectural shapes such as topiary box or bay look smart and stylish in metal buckets, which can be bought for just a few pounds from hardware shops. You can even recycle baked-bean or tomato tins and make them into vases for cut flowers or, with small holes punched in the bottom for drainage, containers for herbs. The Spanish are particularly fond of this idea and use giant olive-oil tins or oil drums to plant everything from geraniums to hollyhocks.

Sky-blue and sea-green plastic pots are an alternative to traditional terracotta. Use as a table decoration or display five or six on a sill.

Based on the design of egg boxes, these functional cardboard seed trays are available from any good garden centre.

For a plain, natural effect, fill an unpainted junk box with silvery thyme and rosemary.

Plain white plastic cups, which can be bought very cheaply from any newsagent or super-market, make useful and simple pots for planting young plants and seedlings.

A window box with picket-fence detail, filled with pots of herbs, is ideal for a kitchen garden.

Wood and plastic

For a rustic look, a basic rectangular window box in strong hardwood like cedar can be left to weather a lovely silvery grey or painted to unify with doors, walls and furniture. It is such fun to pick your own juicy tomatoes and to have a few herbs at hand for giving delicious flavour to suppers of fish, new potatoes and salad. A simple window-box kitchen garden could have herbs like chives and parsley at the back and trailing cherry tomatoes at the front. Or, for a simple, uniform scheme, plant white or blue hyacinths, hedges of dwarf lavender, nasturtiums or white asters. Wooden slatted tubs, barrel shaped or square, can be filled with anything from wild flowers and herbs to topiary box trees or giant sunflowers. Wooden seed trays, filled with pots of herbs, look good displayed on outdoor tables. Steer clear of plastic pots and window boxes in soulless colours and shapes. Be inventive and adapt brightly coloured washing-up bowls and buckets, in vivid greens and blues, from a hardware or discount shop, for a more contemporary look.

Basic and traditional wooden seed trays are a practical and innovative way of displaying pots of flowers or herbs.

An old wooden box has been given a face-lift with coats of white emulsion to make a simple window box for flowers or herbs.

An ugly standard plastic window box has been transformed with two coats of powder-blue emulsion, and then planted with ornamental kale cabbages for a stylish, contemporary look.

Flowers and plants

It is exciting to grow your own flowers, herbs, vegetables and fruits – and you don't have to be an expert. It is equally pleasing to nurture a window box or grow a tub of rocket from seed as it is to plan a large-scale garden. Colour is the most important criterion for me when it comes to choosing flowers and plants. My favourites remind me of childhood summers: white climbing roses; fat purple alliums; white and pinky-purple clematis; pink foxgloves; deep-blue and laven-der delphiniums; blowsy pink peonies; and gaudy orange, pink, white and red dahlias. I am an impatient gardener who wants the picture on the seed packet to be realized overnight. Although it is satisfying to take a cutting of a plant like honeysuckle, stick it in the earth and actually see it start to shoot a few days later, with the constraints of domestic hurly-burly, it is more sensible to invest in young plants from garden centres. When it comes to home-grown produce, it is possible to grow things in confined spaces: I had a good crop of tomatoes this sum-

mer from four or five plants in pots on the roof garden, plus nasturtiums and rocket grown from seed. There are also pots of herbs like basil, mint, thyme and rosemary, just some essentials to have at hand for flavouring every-thing from fish to salads.

Flowers

I am not a serious gardener since colour is my main priority when choosing flowers. I am not concerned with planting fashionable varieties and I probably make dreadful gardening gaffs simply because I want the colours to look right together. I am sure it is not *de rigueur* to mix tomatoes, nasturtiums and white clematis – a group I had on my roof terrace – but against the dreary urban roof-scape of concrete and brick, the bursts of vibrant orange, yellow, scarlet and white on a backdrop of greenery looked cheery. My dream is for a totally white garden (much like my ideal white minimalist interior), scented, romantic and flowering all year. To achieve the former I

need a lot more gardening expertise than I am prepared to gain, and with three children the interior vision is not meant to be – at least for a few years. Therefore, I am content to be less exacting about colour in the garden and to experiment and make mistakes. I stick loosely to a palette of individual colours that also marry well with each other: white, pink, lavender, and hot oranges and yellows. I find that blocks of single colours tend to be more dramatic and less confusing to the eye,

opposite, clockwise from top left *Pretty blue border geraniums; leggy delphiniums to add height; delicate white violas; foxgloves – easy to grow, but most are biennial; agapanthus, with ball-like flowers on slim green stems.*
above *Not all poppies are red; more delicate shades include white, lavender and blue.*
right *Passion flowers are vigorous climbers.*

like a wall smothered with white roses, tubs of green topiary box standards, or a path edged with pinks. For height and drama I love foxgloves, especially white ones. Having disdained this woodland plant for years as a self-seeding weed, gardeners now compete to produce varieties for flower shows in the most subtle shades of pink, white and lavender. The tag that came with my appropriately named 'Albino' describes the majestic spikes of tubular white flowers that bloom during June and July, and, of course, the warning that foxgloves are toxic if eaten. I managed to grow them in large pots on the roof with quite satisfactory results. One day I will plant pots of white agapanthus, whose graceful stems support lacy heads – another good plant for height that grows well in

sunny spots. Delphiniums seem ridiculously easy for amateurs like me to grow and their tall spikes with a froth of blue and mauve flowers exist quite happily in potting composts enriched regularly with bone meal and plant food. Climbing white roses and pot-grown rambling clematis are other favourites that are good for camouflaging unsightly objects. Passion flower is a pretty climber that grows well in sheltered positions. The blooms only last a day or so, but are produced so freely that there is a constant display from June to September, often followed by edible bright-orange

opposite, clockwise from top left *Peonies look beautiful even after heavy rain; voluptuous, rain-soaked summer roses; morning glory's trumpet-like flowers live less than 24 hours.*

clockwise from top left *Poppies look wonderful in wild, uncut grass; border geraniums add a touch of delicacy; woodland foxgloves look at home in both country and urban gardens.*

61

fruit. Morning glory is another eager half-hardy annual that produces myriad trumpet-shaped flowers, in sky blue, magenta or deep pink, from June to September. The flowers last only part of a day, normally closing during early afternoon, but, shaded from the mid-day sun, they may last until evening. A traditional cottage-garden flower with late-summer blooms, often used to edge a path or potato patch, the perennial dahlia is ideally suited to making a brash colour statement. With many varieties and marvellous combinations of white, crimson, pink, yellow and purple – some with two colours in one stem – dahlias are making a comeback in gardening circles. Zinnias are another showy flower in gorgeous orange and pink, with broad and flat, rolled, or even frilled petals. They flower in late summer and give life to a border. While carnations are deemed rather kitsch, the common garden pink, which is in the same family, is a pretty, feathery, old-fashioned border flower, which is easy to grow and maintain.

opposite *Dahlias make bold colour statements.* **clockwise from top left** *A fuchsia-pink dog rose; a feathery petalled dahlia; home-grown nasturtiums; pretty cottage-garden pinks; a vibrant zinnia; poppies growing in long grass.*

Herbs

Herbs look beautiful and taste good: camomile or thyme are fragrant planted between flagstones; mint, thyme and parsley make good cottage-garden borders; and rosemary or bay can be clipped into architectural shapes. Even if you are restricted to a windowsill or balcony it is possible to grow in containers most of the herbs needed for cooking. Flavouring tomato salads and sauces without basil would be dull, and I generally keep a plant in the warmest, most sheltered spot for the duration of summer, and freeze sprigs for use in winter. Sage grows quite happily on the roof terrace and is reasonably hardy. I love the strongly scented leaves chopped sparingly into sauces and salads. Part of the pleasure of growing rosemary is cutting the spikes, which releases the heavenly sharp scent. Used sparingly, rosemary is delicious with pork, chicken and roasted vegetables. Mint has an irresistible smell and flavour, and grows like wildfire. I use tiny sprigs to decorate ice-cream and to add flavour to new potatoes. It is a pleasure to pinch the scented leaves of lemon balm, which is useful to add to wine punches and salads.

clockwise from top left *Basil, delicious in salads and sauces, thrives in sheltered spots but is destroyed by the first hint of frost; lavender looks and smells wonderful and can be used to flavour biscuits; drought-resistant rosemary is deliciously aromatic, but needs to be used sparingly in the kitchen; lemon balm grows vigorously and is delicious in punches; sage keeps its leaves throughout the winter and tastes good in stuffings and stews.*
opposite *Parsely is a versatile herb and is particularly good for flavouring salads.*

Edible flowers

Edible flowers add colour and taste to salads, puddings and cakes. Crystallizing rose petals is a magical way of dressing up fairy cakes or buns. Wash your favourite petals from the garden, dip them in a mixture of egg white and sugar, then leave them to dry. Try crystallizing viola, pansy, geranium and lavender flowers, too. Bonnet-like pansy flowers make short-breads into edible works of art, and bright-orange marigold petals look pretty on top of iced buns. Bright-blue borage flowers, traditionally used in ice-cold Pimm's and lemonade, look pretty on a salad of courgette and cucumber. Both dandelion and nasturtium flowers and leaves make vibrant additions to green salads, and yellow courgette flowers are very tasty if you dip them in a light batter and deep-fry them for a few minutes, and they also look good raw in salads.

opposite, top to bottom
Pansies, borage and crystallized rose petals are pretty decorations for biscuits, salads and cakes.
far right *Fresh herbs and flowers.*

right *Grilled courgettes decorated with courgette flowers; unpicked flowers will become new fruits.*
below *Nasturtium flowers and leaves taste nutty in salads.*

Produce

I have always had a fascination for seed packets and the magnificent specimens that are promised in the illustrations. Even though we lived in London with little room for a vegetable patch, my parents grew courgettes, tomatoes and raspberries covered in bridal-like veiling to keep off the birds. We had two big plum trees, one a Victoria that bent double and eventually collapsed with its yield of fat, juicy plums. My mother was endlessly making jam and there always came a point when my sister and I never wanted to see a plum again. My family and I are learning to grow things using the knowledge of the villagers near our house in Spain. We have learnt how to plant, stake and care for tomatoes, how to dip ridges for potatoes, how to take the seeds out of sunflowers and even how to thresh chickpeas. To cope with a glut of tomatoes, we skin and bottle them to store away for use in the winter in salads and stews. Even though the slugs and some kind of wilt threatened, we cut and ate our own magnificent cabbages which, lightly steamed with butter, even

the under-eights ate without dissent. At home in England, apple trees provide fruit for cooking and eating, and there are plenty of strawberries, raspberries and gooseberries for delicious fools and jams. I have even been successful on my roof terrace this summer with a trailing variety of tomato that grew up wigwams of sticks and produced tasty rosy-red specimens. I have also had luck with rocket, which grows with ease from seed and is a delicious nutty and slightly bitter addition to salads. Wild food is especially fun to collect: blackberries come to mind immediately, and they make delicious jam and pies. Sloes, found in country hedgerows, are bitter raw, but they can be added to gin and left to steep for a few months to make a pink, sweet brew in time for Christmas.

Fabrics and furniture

Toughness and durability are essential qualities for outdoor fabrics and furniture. All-purpose cotton canvas works well for simple chair covers and shady awnings, while cream calico – cheap, durable and washable – is ideal for making table-cloths, loose covers and cushions. Another favourite understated fabric is blue-and-white ticking, a robust cotton twill closely woven in narrow stripes. Traditionally used for pillows and mattresses, it looks good in any setting, whether as cushions on a hot whitewashed patio, or as simple chair covers in a leafy garden. Plasticized cotton or PVC are useful for waterproof tablecloths and come by the metre in checks and bold colours from department stores. You don't have to invest in extra sets of furniture for outside: indoor foldable chairs can be whisked out when the sun shines, as can a lightweight table. If you prefer permanent outdoor furniture, hardwoods should be oiled regularly or coated with tough exterior paint. The alternative is the aged, weath-

ered effect: peeling paint, algae-encrusted wood or rusty metal – organic textures that look at home with outside elements. There are plenty of outlets for junky furniture that can be left outside, but any expensive pieces should be brought inside once summer is over.

Fabrics

Fabrics need to be tough and hard-wearing for outside use. The best textures include canvas, linen and washable plastic. Department stores or haberdasheries are great sources of stripy deck-chair canvas, plasticized cottons for cloths and basic cotton calico. For stylish colours – bright blue, green, pink and orange – head off to interior design shops that update their collections as regularly as fashion houses. Heavy cotton canvas is one of the most adaptable fabrics and can be used to make sturdy loose covers for garden chairs. It is important to wash natural-fibre fabrics before cutting and sewing, so that you can renovate them in the wash without disastrous shrinking. I like to buy tough blue and white plain or striped cotton canvas to make awnings for my yard. The ends are hemmed and the corners punched with metal eyelets (very easy to do with a hole-punching kit). The awning is secured to hooks on the wall with nylon rope that can be adjusted as necessary. White and cream fabrics look fabulous, especially in a white-painted outside space. Imagine that you are creating the outside version of a simple, minimalist interior. White cotton loose covers can disguise ill-matching chairs, and a white sheet flung over a table looks stylish and provides a plain background for food. Scatter cushions should be filled with feathers and bench squabs should be of good-quality foam and have removable covers secured with Velcro, buttons or simple ties. Fabrics in vibrant seaside blues, apple greens and rosy pinks add colour and enhance surrounding flowers and greenery. Pink and orange cloths and napkins look bright and contemporary, while blue-and-white ticking looks smart in any setting and makes understated covers for cushions, bolsters and chairs.

See pages 154–5 for fabric details.

11

12

13

14

27

23

20

15

26

22

6

25

19

24

21

18

17

Furniture

Simple wooden benches of teak or another tough hardwood look good left in their natural state, or they can be painted with exterior paint, like this one in bright cornflower blue.

This contemporary rocking version of a traditional deck chair folds away for easy storage. It has a lightweight aluminium frame and a tough green Textilene cover.

Cheap, practical, but totally charmless, moulded plastic garden furniture has spread like a rash through parks, hotels and gardens. Here are some simple, decorative alternatives for seats and tables that combine form and function without breaking the bank. Anything that folds is useful, so it can be brought inside when the elements become inclement. My favourites are small folding

Solid wooden garden tables are one of the most practical outdoor items and can be put to use at any time of year, with painted surfaces that weather well for an organic look.

Picked up in a junk shop, this old folding metal table with flaking paint looks good in the garden all year, and can be used to display pots of spring bulbs, or laid for summer meals.

A small folding table makes a dining table for one, and two or three can be put together to accommodate more people.

A folding director's chair, with a yellow checked cotton seat and back, is painted a sludgy grey that blends with garden greenery.

A flat-pack pine potting bench has been updated with coats of sea-blue emulsion. Use it to store flowerpots, seed trays and tools, or as a side table for serving food.

A traditional deck chair in a tough blue-and-white checked cotton cover looks crisp and jolly in any outdoor setting.

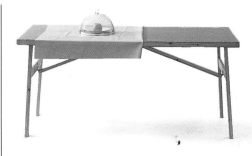

A cheap wood-and-fibreboard folding table can be carried outside for seating large groups of people; it can be smartened up with a cloth in white cotton or bright lime-green PVC.

Lightweight folding cricket chairs are smart for outdoor dining. They come in lots of colours from sea blue to white, and old ones are often nicely worn and have rough, blistered paint.

slatted wooden tables spruced up with a lick of white emulsion each season. There are streamlined, contemporary folding chairs and loungers with lightweight aluminium frames and tough synthetic covers. Outside furniture can be very basic: a plain white cloth on a practical folding decorating table becomes stylish with a couple of jars of cut flowers and some white candles.

A white folding wooden slatted chair with arms has a seaside look; it can be made more comfortable by adding cushions, in blue-and-white ticking, for example.

This sun-lounger is made of aluminium with a Textilene all-weather fabric cover. Ideal for camping, or for stretching out on a sun deck, beside a pool, or in the back garden.

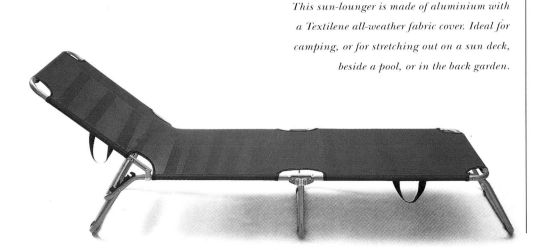

A vibrant lime-green checked cotton deck-chair cover is an alternative to traditional stripes.

Accessories

Kitting out your outside space is no different from furnishing a room inside. The furniture will largely determine the look, so first decide whether to buy smart pieces that need to be stored inside during winter or to look around in junk shops for old metal or wooden tables, benches and chairs that can be left outside to weather and provide exterior detail all year round. A simple solution for outside eating is to buy a hardboard tabletop with separate trestles and folding chairs, which can be dressed up with natural fabrics like cotton, calico, canvas and ticking. There is enormous scope for creating stylish outside table settings. Forget the days when we were expected to lay dinner tables with immaculate sets of cutlery and cut-glass crystal. At the most basic level, unbreakable plastic cups, bowls and plates are useful for children and picnics, while simple white catering china, with enamelled tin bowls and jugs, creates a plain look that can be embellished with jugs of colourful flowers, glowing candles and napkins in brightly coloured checks. I have a passion for old glassware and love to mix odd glasses and jugs found in markets and junk shops. Whatever you choose, the only rule is to try to create informal settings that look wonderful, yet are simply achieved.

Lighting

Without doubt, the most sensuous outside lighting is candlelight at an alfresco supper or the flickering flames of a campfire. The only really pretty electric lights are white fairy lights, like those used on Christmas trees, which look magical strung in rows across a garden or patio. Cream candles are my favourite lights for outside and I have a store of empty jam jars which make really cheap but attractive containers. I also like glass storm lamps and find that a line of three or four along the table creates pools of soft light. Candles can be displayed effectively in basic metal lanterns from hardware shops, which are practical because they can be hung on hooks on the wall. For simple, cheap outdoor lighting buy bags of nightlights in metal holders. They look stylish in flickering groups of two dozen or so in the centre of a table or in lines along window ledges, or placed individually in niches in old walls. Nightlights can burn in a soft breeze but on windy evenings I put them in jam jars or old terracotta pots.

Utensils

A tough white plastic salad bowl is practical for use in the garden and kitchen, and lightweight enough to take on picnics.

A plain wooden tray is ideal for carrying food, drinks and utensils out into the garden. This one has been given a face-lift with blue emulsion.

Dome-shaped food nets conjure up images of old-fashioned country dairies and are efficient at keeping bugs off meat and cheese.

I use simple, basic, functional equipment and utensils for outdoor eating. Invaluable favourites include tough, unbreakable plastic bowls, plates and mugs, which can be bought really cheaply from hardware and chain stores. Tough glassware – such as anything made by Duralex – is not only practical, but looks very smart and is also widely available. For picnics and

If outdoor meals involve children, delicate cups and glasses are likely to end up in smithereens. Play safe with plastic mugs and sturdy Duralex glassware that comes in lots of smart shapes and even bounces when dropped.

Reminiscent of those used in school dining rooms, a simple glass water jug looks good on an outside table, and is very cheap and easy to find in hardware shops.

A basic rectangular plastic lunch box, which can be slipped into a bag or rucksack quite conveniently, is always useful for picnics or for carrying sandwiches to school or work.

Enamelled tin plates and mugs are great camping basics and also look good at the table. You can find this utilitarian tableware in hardware stores and camping shops.

Department stores are good sources of cheap and cheerful, brightly coloured plastic tableware, such as these vibrant orange examples that are ideal for picnics and informal outside meals at home.

A traditional barbecue is good for cook-ups at home or on the beach. Although tiny, it will produce sufficient heat to cook four lamb cutlets with garlic, with enough heat left over to roast bananas in their skins.

Napkins and place mats in bright solid colours or checks look best against plain cloths or bare wooden tabletops, and are cheerful even on the dullest summer's day.

Keep bottles cool with an insulated bottle cooler. This metal one is useful for smaller bottles or for butter and other fast-melting food.

eating on the move I am very fond of my tiny metal barbecue, which gives out enough heat to cook a veritable feast of sausages, or delicious fresh fish, vegetables, and even bananas and marshmallows. Brewing up cups of steaming coffee on a Primus stove with a camping kettle is also a great way of keeping warm when picnicking on a sharp and clear winter's day.

A simple galvanized metal jug gives a robust, utilitarian look to outdoor table settings and is perfect for serving glasses of ice-cold water, or for holding a bunch of freshly cut flowers.

For a truly luxurious picnic, take bottles of drinking water to brew reviving cups of fresh coffee and tea, using an old-fashioned camping kettle heated over an open fire or gas camping stove.

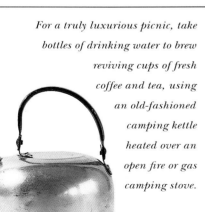

Plain white china is the best neutral backdrop for food, and is the perfect choice for stylish yet simple table settings.

PUTTING IT ALL
TOGETH

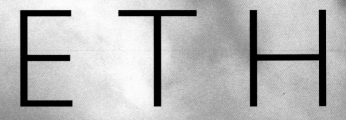

ER

Create a simple, colourful, textural outside retreat, where you can unwind on a heap of soft cushions, or soak up the heady scent of a climbing rose. Get in touch with the elements and plant a vegetable patch to grow your own nourishing produce. Bring your dining room outside for delicious, informal meals, or stretch out on a rug on the grass for a picnic.

Outside retreats

Many of us, especially urban dwellers, are hemmed in for much of the working day and hardly experience fresh air, let alone the sensations of a crisp and frosty morning or the brilliance of a red sunset. Deprived of natural sensations and smells, we humans get depressed, lethargic and irritable, but our sense of wellbeing increases dramatically when we go outside. Whether it is a terrace, patio, vegetable patch, or even a windowsill with a brimming window box, having an outside space to tend to and enjoy creates a diversion from the irritants of daily life – bills, unwanted phone calls, dirty dishes and so on. Making a room outside – somewhere to eat, drink, sit, contemplate, garden, or play – is no different from decorating and furnishing spaces inside our homes. Outside as well as in, it is important to decide what sort of overall look and feel you wish to create and to be resourceful with your available space. The crucial design aspects still apply, such as what colour to paint walls, what kind of floor-

ing and fabric to choose, and what sort of furniture will work. It is also about creating a little bit of magic to give you a wonderful retreat in which to sit with a book on warm summer evenings or eat croissants and drink steaming coffee in the crisp morning air.

An elegant shady Long Island porch is painted white and blue and furnished simply with old wicker tables and chairs, with soft feather cushions covered in faded blue-and-white striped ticking.

below left and right
Porch style in the barn-red cabins of America's Catskill Mountains makes the most of a selection of simple junk furniture.

Verandas and porches

I grew up believing that only television characters whiled away warm velvet-dark evenings in rocking chairs on wooden porches, listening to crickets. When I finally visited the USA I saw that it really happens. I am envious that the long, hot summers have made this simple and practical architectural feature a necessity, as well as being a means of enjoying the outside in comfort. Among the neat picket fences and lawns of New England I saw the most charming porches and verandas with pristine white-painted railings and floors. Often enclosed with fine mesh screens to keep out insects, porches are shady retreats where visitors are refreshed with jugs of iced tea and entertained with stories about wild bears. The most stylish and simple porch furniture are informal old wicker chairs and tables, traditional rocking chairs and hammocks, with cushions in faded blue-and-white stripes. Some of the best furniture has been bought for just a few dollars from junk shops. In the absence of the real thing, the porch look is easy and inexpensive to achieve using stylish old furniture revamped with paint in funky colours and chair covers and cushions in natural fabrics.

above and right
Enclosed with green-painted metal railings, this London roof terrace is a welcome sun-trap, which is ideal for growing toma-toes, pots of herbs and nasturtiums. The look is simple and utilitarian, *with basic tools, old chairs and a table with a green-and-white checked plastic cloth.*
opposite *A blue-and-white checked rug and some big cushions make a white metal bench a more comfortable proposition.*

Rooftop space

It wasn't until the railings were fixed around the flat roof in the back yard of my London house that I felt it was really an outside room. Before, there was always a niggling feeling that someone might topple over and, of course, it was out of bounds for children. Apart from installing an outside tap for watering, which in summer is essential twice a day, the other important task was to lay the pine decking. With a shady courtyard below, the roof is a welcome suntrap, and for that reason I haven't bothered with awnings – on hot days we make do with wide-brimmed hats and sunglasses. To make it more sheltered and secretive, clematis, growing in pots, trails around the railings and over a simple trellis painted with pale minty green emulsion. Mixing vegetables with flowers makes gardening a more productive and resourceful occupation, and I like to grow nasturtiums alongside tomatoes and herbs. Even though the garden is no more than 3.5 square metres, there is a sense of space and freedom among the urban rooftops, and there is nothing better than stealing up there to have a bagel and a coffee on a warm summer's morning.

Beach-hut style

Nearly every seaside town around Britain has a stretch of beach or seafront devoted to higgledy-piggledy strings of small wooden huts that allow you to live, albeit temporarily, in a basic fashion without water or electricity beside the sea. Old-fashioned resorts like Swanage, Bognor, Worthing and Whistable have great beach huts – the best ones are in isolated spots away from the town centres. Colours vary from place to place: jaunty blue and white; dark brown creosote; glorious ice-cream shades of pistachio, raspberry and mint; and plain white are all vernacular beach-hut paint schemes which will inspire you to create the maritime look at home. Collect pebbles from the beach to make simple seaside still lifes and grow plants like sea kale, which thrive on pebbly beaches, for greenery and texture. My grandmother rented a beach hut in Devon for wonderful informal picnics with scratchy sand on the floor and fishing nets in the corner. Beach-hut kit was appropriately simple: jolly blue-and-white striped canvas deck chairs; a folding table; plain cotton cloths; functional picnic gear in a wicker basket; a Primus stove to brew hot drinks; and a warm rug for naps.

opposite

Traditional beach huts, like these at Worthing, give brilliant ideas for painting a shed or furnishing a deck.

above, left to right

Sea kale growing among pebbles is great for creating texture. Paint the walls white and rig up a decorative awning in jolly blue-and-white canvas; for practical, stylish seating, use a white slatted folding chair.

Hot patio

During the long, hot Andalusian summer, all our outside activities take place on the white patio surrounding our house. Rather than opting for rustic limewash, which needs a new coat every spring, we chose basic white matt exterior paint for the walls. The large terracotta tiles underfoot were bought from the local builder's merchant at a very low cost. Furniture is portable so that chairs and tables can be moved according to the time of day. I go to Seville to buy traditional Spanish country chairs and stools with rush seats, which have a timeless appeal. In contrast to the predominately white feel, I like to add splashes of bright colour with shocking-pink napkins or a bright 1940s green-and-turquoise seersucker cloth. Shade is vital, and I designed basic canvas awnings, punched with eyelets and strung to hooks with tough nylon rope.

right *This shady terrace, where the predominance of white is offset by splashes of colourful table linen, is a cool evening retreat.*
opposite *An awning in blue-and-white striped canvas creates shade on the sun-baked patio.*

Urban back yard

A plain, simple and utilitarian approach is the key to creating a stylish summer oasis in the confines of a small urban back yard. Rather than being plastered over or repointed, the rough, uneven brick walls have been left to impart their warm, earthy character, together with the worn mossy red-brick pavers that lie underfoot. This natural, neutral backdrop makes cream canvas chair covers an understandable choice, while a simple white cotton cloth dresses up a folding, rather battered, card table. An old wooden meat safe, a mesh food net, a metal flower bucket and tin lanterns hung on the walls are practical and add hard-edged yet decorative detail. An old metal shoe locker makes an impromptu potting shed, with neat

shelves for storing bulbs, pots and tools. A school-room-style jug, plain bowls and robust glasses are ideal for the uncluttered look. Greenery is sparse apart from clematis and some rampant buddleia, so anything other than the small topiary box and an amaryllis in a roughly moulded terra-cotta pot would be unnecessary.

opposite, left and above
Utilitarian objects like an old wooden meat safe and a metal shoe locker are useful for storing gardening items in the confines of an urban back yard.

above, below and right *Blue-and-white checked table linen, white folding cricket chairs, a vase of pink stocks and a sea-green door add cheerful and contemporary colouring to a shady London courtyard.*
opposite *Instant greenery is provided by a young tomato plant in a terracotta pot and a tall architectural-looking bay standard in a metal bucket.*

Colourful courtyard

A simple way to relieve the drabness of a shady courtyard is to use colourful paint and fabric. I transformed a door with eggshell paint in greenish blue, a colour that is modern, yet fresh and natural. It looked so good that a wall, rebuilt and pointed with ugly cement, was the next contender for the same colour, but in a durable matt emulsion. Ugly water tanks, fences and furniture can also be camouflaged with paint – white is always a good colour to lift a dull, flat environment. Blue-and-white checked cotton is unfailingly cheerful and smart and I used a favourite from my stash of colourful cloths. In a space devoid of many plants, buy colourful flowers like cow parsley, cornflowers or stocks for informal decorations that can be enjoyed outside for several days.

opposite and right *Four gnarled grapevines spread a leafy canopy across the terrace of an Andalusian farmhouse. Bright oranges and pinks for tablecloth, napkins and throw are a perfect match for strong Southern sunlight.*

Vine-covered terrace

A trailing grapevine is a romantic, cool and natural way of shading a terrace. At an ancient Andalusian farmhouse high up among the chestnut and olive groves, four vines, including a knotted and gnarled 20-year-old specimen, have been trained to grow up chestnut posts spaced at 2-metre intervals and across a basic framework of supporting sticks. During the long, hot summers everyone eats lunch and dinner under the vines, which sag with bunches of fat, juicy grapes. In early spring when the vines are not in full leaf, the open spaces are filled in with green fabric awning. Locals say that it takes about three years of careful tending and cutting back to make a fully covered vine canopy. Although a vine outside in a colder climate is unlikely to produce such prodigious fruit, it is possible in a sunny, sheltered, south-facing garden to grow impressive leafy examples. There are some garden specialists who import, at vast expense, 50-year-old vines from the South of France. For outside living an assortment of seats, like old country chairs and benches, together with new metal garden chairs from department stores, creates a relaxed look. When there are guests to feed, more tables can be brought out under the leafy awning.

this page and opposite

Ideas for understated, natural-looking window-ledge gardens: lavender in a painted vegetable crate (bottom); painted plastic window boxes planted with ornamental cabbages (below); blue-painted pots of geraniums (right); and a cedar box with aromatic rosemary (opposite).

Window-box garden

Close to my London home, tubs and pots teeter along the ledges of tower blocks, creating brilliant splashes of colour. These miniature gardens yielding herbs and vegetables, or gaudy favourites like geraniums and marigolds are a vibrant sight in an otherwise grim, unrelenting urban environment. Instead of standard containers, be inventive and revamp an old crate with sludgy green paint and plant textural lavender. Green plastic window boxes look functional, but they can also be transformed with matt paint in soft mint green or powder blue. Don't stick to the same old planting material either: a dwarf hedge of rosemary, white hyacinths, nasturtiums or cherry tomatoes are just some ideas.

Vegetable and flower plot

There is something so satisfying about tending a garden that yields flowers for colour alongside vegetables to eat. This decorative but utilitarian rectangular plot is bordered by a handmade stick fence and yields a combination of floral and edible produce, including clematis, morning glory, sunflowers, lettuces, cabbages, chards and beetroots. In summer, it is a glorious refuge in the cool of early morning or evening, for watering and weeding, soaking up the scents of herbs and enjoying the fresh, bright colours of the young plants.

above *Simple wooden furniture, like a rustic Adirondack chair (left) and a battered junk kitchen chair complete with flaking paint (right), suit this decorative working garden.*

opposite *A mixture of colourful flowers and vegetables grow together in this little enclosed garden in America's Catskill Mountains – a truly peaceful oasis in which to sit and contemplate.*

Planting ideas

All gardeners have their own ideas about the key elements in planting a successful outside space. I view simplicity of layout, together with texture, colour, shape, scent and the edibility of flowers and plants as the most important considerations. I like a sense of order and have a passion for regimented vegetable patches, which have an appeal similar to that of neatly arranged interior rooms. I also like the use of commonplace plants, rather than fancy, exotic varieties that I am happy to leave to real garden experts. Some of my favourites are traditional cottage-garden flowers like roses, dahlias and clematis, as well as all vegetables – especially cabbages, which look so leafy and decorative. The use of containers, from earthy terracotta flowerpots to galvanized metal florist's buckets, is important when space is limited in back yards and on small terraces and balconies. Choosing a pot the right size, painting it a particular colour, and siting it somewhere appropriate are all important. Planting to

create texture and colour with climbing plants, or to make a dramatic architectural statement with tall plants such as sunflowers or topiary trees like box and bay, are also elements that I consider vitally important to creating a living, visually appealing space.

clockwise from near right
Hollyhocks look distinctive against plain white walls; a low white picket fence is bordered by loosestrife for colourful height and detail; sunflowers grow fast and are ideal for creating tall borders; traditionally used for height in herbaceous borders, delphiniums look good in any setting, such as an urban rooftop.
opposite *Leeks that have been left to bolt make a dramatic and decorative architectural statement.*

Creating height

Tall, leggy plants provide drama, height and camouflage. My favourite are sunflowers which are fun to grow from seed; some varieties reach 3 metres or more, with flowers the size of large plates. Another passion, grown in pots against a wall, are foxgloves, which shoot up with ease to over a metre and have pretty white, purple or pink bell-shaped flowers which bees love. Delphiniums are easy to grow and also have colourful spiky blooms. Other tall plants that are easy to grow include hollyhocks, which have a timeless appeal and look pretty flanking a doorway.

A sense of order

There is something pleasing about small-scale plots with neat rows of vegetables and herbs, tidy flowerbeds with an array of foliage and blooms in colours that blend together or contrast dramatically, and well-raked, weeded soil. It proves that humans can contain nature if they methodically dig, plant and tidy. Create natural order in a decorative yet functional garden, with devices such as pathways — wide enough for a wheelbarrow — made of wood chippings and bordered with lacy flat-leafed parsley, and rows of wonderful old glass bell jars to nurture seedlings. Enclose the area with commonplace yet stylish wire fencing over which climbers like honeysuckle and trailing tomatoes can be entwined.

top left and right, and opposite *Meticulous and well-ordered planting in a small ornamental and practical vegetable and flower garden.*
above *A makeshift cold frame constructed from salvaged windows is planted with herbs and salad ingredients.*

Potting ideas

A terracotta pot is hard to beat as a container for everything from bulbs to shrubs and herbs. The earthiest pots are the old roughly moulded hand-thrown ones that are more textural than machine-produced models. Interesting containers are not difficult to find. Raid your local hardware shop for galvanized metal buckets, which look great with topiary standards of box, bay or rosemary, but drill holes for drainage. Bear in mind that often the simplest arrangements of only two or three pots can be the most effective. Galvanized troughs look functional and modern on windowsills planted with pretty flowers like narcissi, hyacinths, ornamental cabbages or herbs.

this page As long as it has an earthy, organic look, almost anything will do as a container for plants and flowers, from galvanized metal troughs or an old sink – either for plants or for a makeshift pond – to traditional terracotta pots. *opposite* Metal buckets from a hardware shop look effective in small groups.

opposite, clockwise from far left *Plumbago climbing up wire; a moss rose trained with string and wire; climbing runner beans; nasturtiums growing up pea sticks.*
left *Clematis and other climbers trail over chicken wire, creating a leafy paradise for hens.*
below *Stick fencing supports trailing tomatoes.*

Climbers

Train climbing plants with wire and garden string along walls, fences and trellis, and up pergolas, arbours and wigwam-shaped structures. As well as creating colour and greenery in a skyward direction, climbers are useful for camouflaging unattractive surfaces. I grow clematis in pots, which runs rampant over the railings around my roof garden and trails up trellis over a section of harsh red-brick wall. The plants soften the hard urban landscape, and exist very well in terracotta pots if they are fed regularly with manure and watered copiously. Other favourite climbers include plumbago, which has beautiful star-like flowers; roses like *Rosa* 'Madame Alfred Carrière' and *R.* 'New Dawn'; gapevines, which are perfect for making shady arbours; jasmine, especially varieties that produce the most wonderful heady scent at night; and passion flowers – I love the purplish blooms and orange fruits. Climbers are also handy if space is short. In a vegetable plot, for example, courgettes, tomatoes, cucumbers, nasturtiums and runner beans can all be trained up stakes and along fences.

Flowers and vegetables

For economic reasons, traditional cottage gardens always contained a mixture of flowers for cutting and vegetables for consumption by the family. Many gardeners, who are not necessarily interested in self-sufficiency, adopt the same approach for purely decorative reasons, since many vegetables and herbs hold ornamental appeal. Others, who enjoy eating the fruits of their labours, delight in growing a combination of the decorative and the edible, with everything from potatoes and beans to roses and sweet peas jostling for position in one patch. I look forward to late summer when tiny plots are ablaze with colour in the form of big, floppy green cabbages and lettuces, together with dahlias in gaudy pinks, yellows and oranges. For dramatic contrast, plant round-headed lettuces next to tall, gangly alliums with their pom-pom flower heads. A combination of parsley chives and mint can be used to create pretty, textural border edgings and the layers of straw mulch, which is used for keeping the soil warm, also look decorative. Tall climbing plants like beans, tomatoes and cucumbers are unusual ideas for attractive green perimeters.

opposite *Floppy green cabbages planted with brilliant dahlias in a London allotment garden are good examples of combined floral and edible produce.*

left and above *This ornamental flower and vegetable patch in the Catskill Mountains in America measures just 6.5 x 9 metres. It is bisected with hard-earth pathways and planted with neat rows of lettuces, chards and cabbages, interspersed with colourful blooms like daisies and marigolds.*

117

right *An apple tree from an espaliered row enclosing a simple vegetable and herb garden.*

opposite, clockwise from top left *A wigwam-shaped wire topiary frame for climbing plants like ivy, nasturtiums, vine tomatoes or beans; as the plant grows, the stems can be trained around the wire and tied in place with string. An aromatic rosemary standard is trimmed into an architectural shape – the clippings can be dried for use in cooking. A squat box ball looks good on its own or arranged with others on a balcony or terrace.*

Clipped and trained

When we think of topiary it is usually yew hedges clipped into the amusing shapes of dogs, cats, chickens, or another favoured animal. On a smaller scale – available from any good garden centre – there are evergreen shrubs like box and bay clipped into squat balls or taller, leggy stems with pom-pom tops. These all look good in small paved areas and require very little maintenance apart from watering and regular trimming with shears to keep them in shape. There are topiary wire frames in wigwam and ball shapes that are good for training things like vine tomatoes, beans and nasturtiums. In the walled gardens of old country houses, you often see the espaliered branches of exotic pear and apple varieties that have been trained to grow flat and spread out in fan shapes. An espalier framework is made with a series of upright posts supporting several wires strained horizontally to secure the branches. An espalier-trained tree is restricted to pairs of branches that stretch out horizontally from the trunk and are secured to the espalier for support. Espaliered trees also make an unusual natural fence or partition in a small garden.

Eating

Eating and drinking are sensual pleasures, and become more so if the ingredients are delicious and the surroundings heavenly. Simplicity is the key to making the most of a balmy evening or a sunny afternoon. Invest in good, basic cooking tools, such as sharp knives, solid mixing bowls and pans with heavy bases. Keep tableware simple with plain white china and durable but good-looking glassware — something like Duralex is perfect. Use white sheets for everyday tablecloths, but for special occasions splash out on beautiful crisp linen. Buy the best cheese, fish, meat, fruit, vegetables and wine that you can afford, and prepare meals that involve minimal preparation. Serve lots of healthy salads and raw vegetables and enjoy experimenting with the addition of home-grown herbs. Set the table in a sheltered, shady environment and keep furniture basic and portable: a trestle table and folding director's chairs are ideal. At night, light candles in lanterns, jam jars or glass holders, and decorate the table with jugs of

freshly cut herbs or flowers such as roses or marigolds. Keep picnic equipment to a minimum, with a cool box, rug and corkscrew. Set up camp under a tree or in a sheltered sand dune and build a fire to cook sausages or pack plenty of bagels and good chocolate and wine.

opposite *A picnic by the sea on the deck of a beach hut is simple and stylish with a white folding chair, blue-and-white napkins and a practical big straw picnic basket.*

right *A perfect picnic: hunks of cucumber; eggs frying on a campfire; and bread with fresh crab.*

Picnics

My family are enthusiastic picnickers who relish the freedom of eating informally outside at any time of year. We head off to Regent's Park or Hyde Park in London, or, when we need to blow away the cobwebs, further afield to a safe, sandy beach such as Camber Sands in Sussex or Studland Bay in Dorset. The best picnics are simple and uncomplicated affairs. For meals by the sea, I pack up a basket with blue-and-white striped napkins, a box of matches and a bottle cooler. In a sheltered spot by a breakwater or in a dune, we make a campfire with driftwood and dried seaweed or light a little metal barbecue for a cook-up after a dip in the sea. Fried eggs or sausages are wedged between chunks of good chewy bread. Sometimes we buy a local dressed crab, which, seasoned with lemon and pepper, we spread onto whole-meal brown bread. On cold but bright winter days, I pack a warm woolly tartan rug, bars of really good chocolate, a flask of potato and leek soup, and a box of smoked salmon and cream cheese bagels. Other picnic goodies include wedges of delicious cheeses with oatcakes and cheese straws, chunks of pinky red tomatoes dipped in a little salt, a jar of olives, large hunks of cucumber and some crisp apples.

above and opposite Simple
food to suit the pared-
down look, with a white
cloth, basic tableware,
practical but attractive
mesh food nets, candles in
glass holders and a few
stems of tuberose, which
smell heavenly at night.
right Roasted peppers
and aubergines; roast
diced potatoes; tomatoes
with olive oil and basil.

Simple supper

I have a passion for vegetables, especially roasted, and find them one of
the simplest, tastiest accompaniments
to grilled or barbecued fish and meat.
For summer suppers, I chop up potatoes, complete with skins, aubergines,
red peppers, onions and courgettes,
and place them in a flat roasting pan
with a good douse of olive oil and
lemon juice, some garlic, rosemary or

basil, and cook them in the middle of a hot oven, turning regularly, for about 45 minutes or until everything is soft and nicely browned. Any leafy green vegetable, such as cabbage, is delicious steamed, then cooked for a minute or so in butter and mint. Staples like baked potatoes, impaled on a skewer for faster cooking, are another favourite served with butter, salt and pepper. Salads of lettuce, rocket or other seasonal leaves are essential, as are home-grown tomatoes, chopped up with basil, garlic, salt, lemon juice and olive oil. In keeping with my pared-down approach to cooking, I cover the table with a crisp white cloth and serve food in large white enamelled metal dishes, which look stylish alongside simple plain white crockery.

Lunch break

When I am dashing about for work, grabbing sandwiches to eat on the run, I think wistfully of my Spanish friends who sit down daily to a relaxing and civilized lunch, either at home where they tuck into something like a tortilla, or in a bar that serves delicious tapas of squid or fried fish. Things are happily different on holidays when there is time to sit down to eat and talk in the middle of the day. Pasta is the top request in my household and, as long as there is a good bed of steaming *al dente* spaghetti to mix the sauce in, I can get away with serving ingredients that are otherwise unacceptable to the youngest members, such as strong cheese, herbs and, worst of all, lots of garlic. Tomato sauce, made with tasty home-grown or field tomatoes, is one of the easiest and most delicious things to serve with pasta. Simply fry three or four large, peeled, chopped tomatoes in olive oil and garlic until they are half cooked. Seasoned with parsley or basil, this highly aromatic, slightly crunchy, tomato sauce is best with a long pasta like tagliatelle or spaghetti. As soon as pumpkins are available in late summer, I cook a kilo or so of the chopped flesh in salted water until soft. After draining, I fry it in olive oil and garlic for a few minutes, and then add half a small pot of single cream, 30 grams of grated Parmesan, and some nutmeg or basil to bring out the flavour of the pumpkin. Then, if I can be bothered, I pulverize the mixture in a blender. When heated up, this utterly delicious pale-orange sauce can be served with any pasta. Fresh wild mushrooms cooked in butter, garlic and parsley are another delicious accompaniment for pasta. Lasagne is also a top-ten favourite, and, instead of minced beef, I sometimes use cooked courgettes, aubergines and tomatoes in between layers of béchamel sauce, pasta sheets and grated Parmesan.

above, left and opposite
Make simple lunch-time pasta treats with chopped home-grown tomatoes and herbs, served with a wedge of fresh bread and a glass of cold white wine.

Birthday party

It is wishful thinking to imagine that junk food like crisps, sweets and fizzy drinks are not expected at a children's party. When my daughter requested pizza for her sixth birthday party, I felt mean when I refused her the bought kind that ooze preservatives, which she had set her sights on. So I was faced with the challenge of producing healthy pizza that would please a disgruntled birthday girl. I cut thick slices of crusty bread and toasted them on one side. Then I rubbed the uncooked side with garlic, trickled on olive oil, and added cooked chopped tomatoes. I topped the slices with grated Parmesan and placed them under the grill until bubbling — a great success. I gave in and bought bottles of the least violently coloured lemonade, but offered jugs of iced water, too, which were just as popular. I also served slices of watermelon and orange, cold from the fridge. We made an outrageously rich chocolate biscuit cake, which was decorated with blackberries and candles. Rather than using plain paper plates and cups, I bought brightly coloured plastic plates, cups and straws from a local discount shop, and laid the table with a length of bright-blue plastic cloth.

opposite, left and above

*Chocolate biscuit cake
and home-made pizza
are key ingredients for a
children's birthday party.
Practical plastic for the
tablecloth, plates, beakers
and straws is available in
lots of bright, cheerful
colours that create a fun
table setting.*

Tea time

A glorious summer's afternoon is a wonderful excuse to make something sticky and sweet to eat outside in the shade, under a tree or on the terrace, with a cup of steaming and refreshing Earl Grey tea. Make this indulgent treat a vibrant occasion with a jazzy orange tablecloth and a jug of bright marigolds, zinnias or roses. For a traditional English tea, make bite-size cucumber and cream cheese sandwiches. Bake some fairy cakes – they really are very simple and quick to make. Mix together 125 grams caster sugar, 2 eggs and 175 grams self-raising flour, then spoon heaped teaspoons of the mixture into little paper cases or greased bun tins and bake at 180°C (350°F), gas mark 4, for ten minutes. When the cakes are cool, decorate them with icing and fresh or crystallized flower petals, like pansy, rose, marigold, nasturtium, geranium, lavender and borage (see page 66). Other tea-time goodies include freshly baked scones, which can be thrown together in a matter of minutes. Simply mix 250 grams self-raising flour, 50 grams butter, 50 grams caster sugar, 1 beaten egg and 75 ml milk in a bowl. Roll out the dough, cut it into rounds, then place them on a greased baking tray and cook at 230°C (450°F), gas mark 8, for ten minutes. Try serving them warm with crème fraîche and home-made blackberry jam. Flapjacks, made with golden syrup, butter and rolled oats, are deliciously chewy, and another favourite are slabs of crumbly shortbread, especially good fresh from the oven.

above *Delicious fairy cakes decorated with icing and fresh marigold petals.*
opposite *A vibrant tea-time table setting with contemporary colour provided by the pink and orange tablecloth, napkins and wool throw. A vase of marigolds and roses adds an extra brilliant touch of colour.*

left *Pale blue-and-white stripes combined with minty green is a stylish and understated colour scheme that is perfect for eating out on a wooden veranda. The folding director's chairs are covered in tough canvas and can be stored away easily at the end of summer. Simple metal hurricane lanterns, and jugs of blue scabious and cornflowers complete the simple, relaxed effect.*
opposite *Ideas for tasty summer puddings include raspberry jellies in chunky 1930s-style glasses that were picked up for a few pence in a junk shop, and a plum tart, which is delicious served with a scoop of crème fraîche.*

Summer puddings

With so many fruits in season – strawberries, cherries and gooseberries – making puddings for summer meals has endless possibilities and can be really simple. My favourite fruit fool, made with thick cream or low-fat fromage frais, is good old-fashioned gooseberry, which I serve with shortbread; other successful fools include lemon, quince and blackberry. Tarts are always a good idea, and, made with plums, peaches or apples in a rich, buttery pastry case like *pâte sucrée*, are delicious hot or cold. Real fruit jellies made with gelatine and fresh raspberry, strawberry, peach or grape juice, look really pretty in individual glasses. There is also traditional basin-shaped summer pudding, perfect for when all the berry fruits are in season, like red and black currants, raspberries and blueberries.

Breakfast

Good coffee, fresh bread, butter and home-made jam are my essentials for a civilized breakfast. I like to make strong Italian espresso coffee in an old-fashioned percolator, and, unless the bread is still warm from the bakery, I prefer it heated up in the oven or toasted. There are so many fancy breads to choose from nowadays, but toasted hunks from a healthy wholemeal loaf or a crusty white loaf are as tasty as they are filling. Breakfast time is a chance to indulge in eating natural honey and home-made jams and marmalades. When bitter Seville oranges are in season in January, I always promise myself I will make a batch of marmalade, which, interestingly, the Spanish themselves don't eat and consider it a curious British habit. Fresh fruit on the table — figs, watermelon, peaches and apples in the summer, and fat, juicy oranges in the winter — is always a treat, and an easy alternative source of vitamin C is a large glass of unsweetened orange juice. Unless it is the weekend or a holiday, I like breakfast to be a fairly quick and efficient meal, with basic white plates and mugs set on a practical, yet jolly, plastic checked cloth.

opposite, above and right

An alfresco breakfast of fresh fruit, bread and honey, washed down with a cup of strong black coffee, is a perfect way to start the day. Simple white plates and mugs set on a practical plastic cloth are also key elements, while shade is provided by home-made canvas awnings.

Mood

It might sound like a cliché, but it invigorates the senses to be outside, in touch with nature and the elements that surround you: water, light, scent and texture. It is delicious to be in the garden after a terrific rain storm, feeling the cool, damp air and seeing leaves glistening with water, or rose petals plastered to the ground like wet confetti. On long, hot, sunny afternoons, any shady spot becomes a welcome retreat, and it is a luxury to lie in dappled light under a tree, eating an ice-cream or enjoying a lazy picnic. Gardens smell of so many things: fragrant roses and honeysuckle; aromatic herbs like rosemary and lavender, which are very hardy and can be grown just about anywhere; and the heady aroma of damp earth after a storm. Scents are evocative of a time and place, and the fragrance of cut grass or a particular rose can take me back to my childhood. When temperatures soar, the mere sound of water – a tinkling fountain or a gushing outdoor shower or tap – are a relief to a hot and bothered body. Try to find the time to hide away outside in the same way as you might curl up with a good book in a comfortable chair by the fire. Take breakfast outside on a warm and sunny summer's morning, or stretch out on a rug on the grass to catch up with a novel.

Lazy afternoon

Looking back to my childhood, I recall days when we walked to the common and ate ice-creams on a rug under a leafy tree. The parade of shops opposite, their stripy blinds lowered, took on a sleepy feel. Afternoons were long and languid, and best spent in the dappled cool of the large apple tree in our garden reading, drinking lemonade and eating biscuits. Squinting at the afternoon sun from my shady retreat under the awning at our house in Spain, time has passed, but the feeling is the same. With echoes of those carefree days, it is an unsurpassed luxury to soak up the enveloping warmth and enjoy a long, lazy lunch of salads, fresh bread and hunks of cheese.

left and opposite

On a long, hot summer's afternoon, keep cool in the dappled light of a shady tree and enjoy a lazy, informal lunch, with plenty of healthy salads, crispy bread and fresh juicy fruit.

right Tranquility in a rain-soaked London garden, with rose petals plastered to the ground and the greenery enlivened and intensified in colour.
below Alchemilla bent double with glistening drops of water.

Rain-soaked garden

Sometimes the summer air becomes stuffy and oppressive. The heat intensifies until you feel the first twinges of a headache; you drink litres of water; clothes feel tight and uncomfortable, and it becomes an effort to attempt the simplest chore. Outside, the air draws closer and the light assumes a dull, flat quality. In the garden there is a sense of anticipation; nothing stirs, and the plants seem stifled by the lack of breeze. The air is thick with the dry, scorched smells of grass and earth. The storm clouds gather and darken, and when the first droplets of rain splash and scatter the dusty surface there is a sense of relief. First one drop, then another, and then the sky empties itself like a giant bucket. The thunder rumbles and roars and lightning snakes through the sky. Heavy rain is wonderfully cleansing and leaves the garden sparkling with wetness. It is intoxicating to walk among the dripping plants and drink in the moist, heady, earthy air. Under bare feet the soaking grass feels spongy, cool and more accommodating. Vegetation is greener, and leaves and petals are shiny like pebbles washed by the tide, and the wet paths house small light-reflecting pools. Serious gardeners dread summer storms, which mostly arrive when gardens are at their peak. Yet although it may be disastrous for prize blooms, voluptuous flowers, with drooping petals ready to fall, assume a fragile rain-sodden beauty after being buffeted and bruised by the elements.

Scent

The intoxicating smell of rambling roses, heady jasmine, or the lingering sweetness of cut tuberoses are, like all garden smells, evocative of a time and place. From my childhood I particularly remember the golden *Rosa* 'Peace' blooms in our garden, which smelt like delicious soap; the fresh, sweet hay-like scent of newly cut grass; and the strange herby smell that lingered on your hands after picking tomatoes. Some of the most aromatic plants are lavender, thyme, camomile and rosemary. Lavender is a hardy evergreen that is easy to grow in pots, or as a decorative hedge or border edging. The spiky stems with delicate purple flowers are typical of summer and smell delicious when brushed against. Lavender can be hung in bunches to dry and the flowers used to fill cotton

bags to scatter among clothes in drawers. Lavender is also useful for giving scent and bulk to potpourri. Hardy thyme and camomile are pretty, compact plants that are easy to grow between paving stones and emit fresh, herby fragrances when crushed underfoot. A carpet of camomile on an area of lawn is another delicious way to impart scent. Thyme is a valuable herb for flavouring meat and fish, while camomile makes a delicious tea. Rosemary is another wonderfully aromatic plant that is easy to grow and looks pretty either as low hedges, in pots or clipped into topiary standards. I dry stems of rosemary and hang them by the oven for flavouring everything from pasta to chicken. I also use jugs or vases of fresh rosemary stems to decorate summer tables.

opposite far left *Thyme planted in cracks between paving stones is a simple way to add soft greenery and a delicious scent when crushed underfoot.*
left and opposite *Lavender is aromatic while it is growing, and the dried flowers can be used in sachets for drawers and in potpourri mixes.*

above *Nestling in the shade of an olive tree, a lightweight folding chair, dressed in a simple cotton pull-on loose cover, makes a peaceful retreat – the perfect place to enjoy a quiet hour or two catching up with your novel.*

right *A shady patch of grass, beneath leafy branches strung with metal candle lanterns, is furnished with a traditional moss-encrusted wooden bench. Next to it, on an old metal table spread with a pink-and-white checked cotton cloth, are bowls of radishes for healthy nibbling.*

Simple retreats

Caught up in the demands of work and domestic life in an age that demands our immediate reaction to every bleep of a pager or fax transmission, it is important to find time and space to sit, reflect, read a book, or do nothing but soak up the beauty of a warm evening. Make your own peaceful retreat with a favourite chair in the most sensuous part of your garden: by a scented rose, perhaps, or in a spot that gets lots of sun, or in a patch of wild grass and flowers. Set up a table and eat lunch there — a sandwich full of good things like grilled vegetables or crisp lettuce leaves and tasty cheese, with fresh strawberries to follow. My place to hide away from daily demands is my tiny rooftop garden, which is cool and refreshing in the early morning and the perfect place to enjoy breakfast with the radio and newspaper. In the middle of the day I can stretch out on a rug on the decking and soak up some warm sunshine. At dusk I like to watch the sky turn pink, light some candles and relish the peace, which is shattered only from time to time as an ambulance or police car shrieks towards another urban calamity.

Top *Simple folding chairs in pretty colours are practical for use in the house and outside, and they are easy to carry to a favourite patch of garden to sit in comfort among wild flowers and uncut grass.*

bottom left and right
A traditional bench painted a basic garden green can be equipped with cushions for extra comfort.

Water

It is refreshing to cool off in the heat of the day with an invigorating swim or cold shower. In the scorching mid-day sun, even the sound of water is a relief to a hot, sticky body. It makes life so much easier if you can install a tap outside for watering plants and to fill bowls of refreshing water to splash you down or soak your feet and hands when the heat becomes too intense. Few of us have the available space or funds required for a swimming pool, but an outside shower is a reasonably inexpensive luxury. Freestanding or fixed to a wall or fence, a simple shower head with a wooden deck beneath is the perfect way to make you feel as if you've just had a reviving dip.

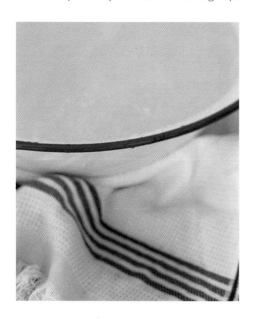

above and right

Install an outside shower to refresh yourself in the height of summer. For maximum style, choose simple, functional shapes for shower heads and pipes, mount them on a wall or fence tucked away in a secluded corner, and plan a suitable surface for drainage, such as a ceramic shower tray or hardwood teak decking.

opposite *Keep cool with an outside tap, such as this one which was bought cheaply from a builder's merchant. As well as making watering easy, you can make an impromptu outside wash-ing area with a simple metal bowl, a soft towel and your favourite soap.*

Shady summer's evening

On a balmy evening, move outside to watch the softening light, lengthening shadows and intensifying hues of a technicolour sunset. As dusk falls, it is a peaceful time to sit and reflect on the day's activities. In keeping with this tranquil mood, make your outdoor room a calm oasis furnished in neutral whites and creams. These colours are my favourites for fabrics and furniture on the patio of our house in Spain, where evenings in summer are spent enjoying the fragrant warm air. The table is laid with candles in metal lanterns and vases of tuberoses, and I bring out cream canvas director's chairs, which are really comfortable for lazing in. We light the barbecue, load it with fish steaks and make simple salads of tomatoes and green leaves. In the courtyard, which is lit with more candles in jam jars and lanterns, bench seating is covered with assorted cushions in plain and blue-and-white striped canvas – ideal for stretching out on after a hearty supper.

right *Neutral fabrics on the terrace at dusk.*
opposite *Soft cushions to relax on, in white and understated stripes.*

right *Picnic on the grass with a blue and white theme on a sunny late-summer's afternoon: a crisp checked cotton cloth, and deck chairs covered in cheerful plain and striped cotton.*

opposite *Pack up a picnic tea in a traditional metal lunch box and choose tea-time favourites like flapjacks, bagels and jam, or slabs of fruitcake.*

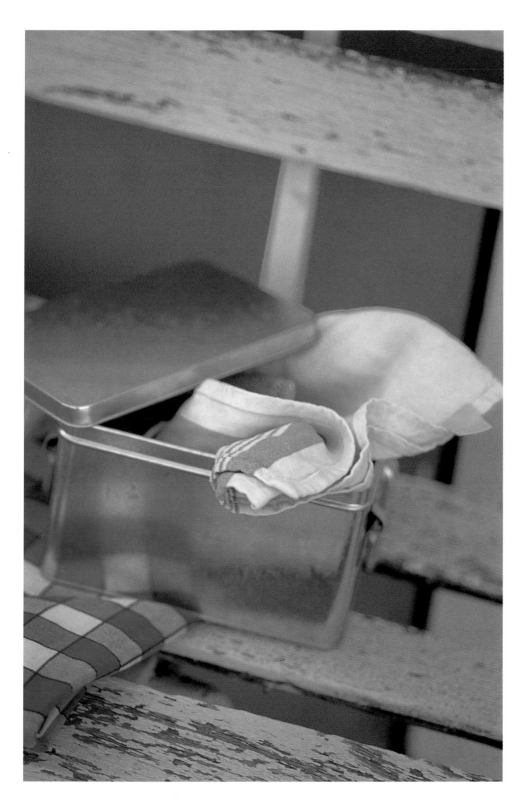

Soft grass

Grass is the perfect outdoor surface for lying on and gazing up at a cloudless summer sky. It comes in many guises: a luxurious stretch of immaculately tended, manicured green lawn, a scorched and bristly playing field, a lush uncultivated field of tall swaying grasses and poppies, or a clipped and cosseted cricket pitch. It is good to feel grass between your toes, or tickling your hands as you idly pick clover and daisies to make into chains. Then there is the wetness of grass early in the morning, glistening with silvery drops of dew, or the soft dampness of a refreshed lawn after a summer rain storm. Pitching camp on a patch of soft, spongy grass is one of the most relaxing ways to spend a hot afternoon at the weekend, and a long, languid picnic will invigorate the soul and improve your mood after the stresses of the week. Some of the best experiences are to be had on a visit to a local park, where you can nearly always find a welcoming shady tree or a secluded sunny patch. Essentials for picnics on the grass are a good cloth to lay your food on and a woolly rug or, if you prefer, some lightweight deck chairs on which to sit.

Credits

1030, Dulux Definitions; deck chair, Jerry's Home Store; folding table, IKEA; old deck chair in green cotton check, Designers Guild; sun-lounger with aluminium frame, Graham & Green.

Pages 78–9

Jug, Ruby Beets Antiques, USA.

Page 80

Clockwise from top right: glass storm lamps, Jerry's Home Store; nightlight, IKEA; lantern, B'zar; hurricane lantern, Jerry's Home Store; candles, Price's Patent Candle Co; glass storm lamp, The Dining Room Shop.

Page 82

Clockwise from top left: white plastic bowl, Divertimenti; wooden tray, Habitat, painted in Sanderson Spectrum 23–05 Easter Egg; plastic mug, Debenhams; Duralex glass, The Conran Shop; tin plate, Blacks Camping Shop; plastic lunch box, Divertimenti; water jug, Staines Catering Equipment; food net, Divertimenti.

Page 83

Clockwise from top left: plastic plate, knife and fork, Woolworth's; Greek barbecue, Young & D; gingham paper napkins, Paperchase; orange-and-pink checked napkin, Designers Guild; metal jug, Jerry's Home Store; white bowl, Staines Catering Equipment; kettle, stylist's own; bottle cooler, Blacks Camping Shop.

Page 86–7

Chairs and cotton covers, The Conran Shop.

Page 88

Blue-and-white striped cotton cushion covers, Ralph Lauren Home Collection, USA; location (top): house of Ellen O'Neill, Long Island, NY, USA; location (bottom left and right): house of Dean Riddle,

Phoenicia, NY, USA.

Page 89

House of Ellen O'Neill, Long Island, NY, USA.

Page 90

Metal sieve, After Noah; chair and wooden trellis painted in Sanderson Spectrum 39–03 Salad Green; checked plastic fabric tablecloth, John Lewis; watering can, Tobias and the Angel.

Page 91

Blue checked wool blanket, Melin Tregwynt.

Page 94

Blue-and-green cloth, Tobias and the Angel; jug, The Conran Shop; folding cricket chairs, Habitat.

Page 95

Wooden folding table, Habitat.

Page 96

Folding chairs, Habitat, with covers made in cotton duck from Whaleys Ltd; food net, Divertimenti; wooden food safe, After Noah.

Page 97

Metal shoe locker, After Noah.

Page 98

Cloth in blue checked cotton, Designers Guild; white bowl, The Conran Shop.

Page 99

Metal bucket, IKEA; bay tree, Clifton Nurseries.

Page 100–1

Garden of Nick and Hermione Tudor, Finca El Moro, Spain.

Page 102

Plastic window boxes, Clifton Nurseries, painted in powder blue emulsion by Farrow & Ball.

Page 103

Cedar window box, Clifton Nurseries; location: house of David and Carolyn Fuest, London.

Page 104–5

Vegetable and flower plot of Dean

Riddle, Phoenicia, NY, USA.

Page 108

Location (bottom right): allotment garden of John Matheson, London.

Page 109

Blue bench, IKEA.

Page 110

Vegetable and flower garden of Nancy McCabe, northwest Connecticut, USA.

Page 112

Metal buckets, IKEA and G J Chapman; small metal bin, Paula Pryke Flowers.

Page 113

Metal planters, The Conran Shop.

Page 115

Chicken coop in the garden of Nancy McCabe, northwest Connecticut, USA; stick fencing in the garden of Dean Riddle, Phoenicia, NY, USA.

Page 117

Vegetable and flower garden of Dean Riddle, Phoenicia, NY, USA.

Page 118

Herb and vegetable garden of Nancy McCabe, northwest Connecticut, USA.

Page 120

Glasses, El Corte Ingles, Spain; food net, Divertimenti.

Page 124

Food nets, Ruby Beet Antiques, USA; storm lamps, Habitat; jug and bowl, The Conran Shop; metal flower bucket, The Conran Shop.

Page 127

Folding cricket chairs and wooden folding tables painted in white emulsion, Habitat.

Page 128–9

Tablecloth in blue PVC fabric from Habitat; straws, IKEA.

Page 130

Checked rug and checked napkins, Designers Guild; cloth in orange

cotton fabric from The Conran Shop.

Page 132

Metal hurricane lanterns, Jerry's Home Store; metal jug, Jerry's Home Store; striped cloth and napkins, Jerry's Home Store; folding chairs, Old Town.

Page 133

Jelly glasses, After Noah; tray, Habitat, painted in Sanderson Spectrum 23–05 Easter Egg.

Page 134

White plates, IKEA.

Page 136–7

Garden of Vanessa de Lisle, Fashion Consultant, London.

Page 138–9

Garden of Lisa Bynon and Mona Nehrenberg, Sag Harbor, NY, USA.

Pages 140–1

Garden of Vanessa de Lisle, Fashion Consultant, London.

Page 144

Cloth in checked cotton by Designers Guild.

Page 146

Bowl and cotton towel, The Conran Shop.

Page 147

Location (right): garden of Lisa Bynon and Mona Nehrenberg, Sag Harbor, NY, USA.

Page 148

Folding director's chairs, Heal's.

Page 149

White folding table painted in white emulsion, Habitat; cushions in bold striped cotton by Laura Ashley and narrow striped cotton by Ian Mankin.

Page 150

Checked cloth, Divertimenti.

Page 151

Metal lunch box, Muji.

Page 152–3

Vegetable and flower garden of Dean Riddle, Phoenicia, NY, USA.

Suppliers

Contact the branches given below for information on local outlets.

Clothes

Old Town, 32 Elm Hill, Norwich, Norfolk NR3 1HG
No-nonsense cotton, moleskin, flannel and Harris tweed; shirts, jerkins and jackets.

Presents for Men, PO Box 16, Banbury, Oxfordshire OX17 1TF
Thick wool fingerless mittens, with thermal insulated lining.

Containers

Catalan Classics, Patch Park Farm, Ongar Road, Abridge, Romford, Essex RM4 1AA
Hand-thrown pots from Catalonia, Spain.

The Chelsea Gardener, 125 Sydney Street, London SW3 6NR
Terracotta, plastic and wood, pots, urns and window boxes.

Classic Gardens, Lower Puncheston, Haverfordwest, Pembrokeshire SA62 5TG
Troughs and handmade window boxes.

Clifton Nurseries, 5a Clifton Villas, London W9 2PH
Everything for a well-furnished garden, an enormous range of terracotta, plus simple window boxes in solid cedar and metal.

Pots and Pithoi, The Barns, East Street, Turners Hill, West Sussex RH10 4QQ
Beautiful selection of handmade terracotta urns made by potters in Crete. Also a good collection of old worn examples.

Fabric

Anta, Fearn, Tain, Ross-shire IV20 1XW
Brilliantly coloured tartans, hard-wearing fringed picnic rugs and blankets.

Laura Ashley, 256–8 Regent Street, London W1R 5DA
Wide selection of coloured cottons and simple blue-and-white stripes or checks.

The Blue Door, 77 Church Road, London SW13 9HH
Blue-and-white Swedish checks, stripes and plains in cotton and linen.

Manuel Canovas Ltd, 2 North Terrace, Brompton Road, London SW3 2BA
Larger-than-life floral cotton prints that look great in bright southern light.

The Conran Shop, Michelin House, 81 Fulham Road, London SW3 6RD
Brightly coloured Indian cottons plus wide range of cotton in whites and creams.

Designers Guild, 267–71 & 277 King's Road, London SW3 5EN
Bright cottons in florals and checks, plus good selection of whites and creams, for tablecloths, loose covers, deck-chair covers, cushions, bolsters and awnings.

Habitat, 196 Tottenham Court Road, London W1P 9LD
Plain, checked and striped cottons for simple loose covers for director's chairs.

Cath Kidston, 8 Clarendon Cross, London W11 4AP
Bright floral 1950s-inspired cotton vinyl for hard-wearing cloths.

Ralph Lauren Home Collection, Selfridges, 400 Oxford Street, London W1A 1AB
Blue-and-white striped cotton fabrics.

Liberty, 214–20 Regent Street, London W1R 6AH
Wide range of furnishing fabrics.

MacCulloch & Wallis, 25–6 Dering Street, London W1R 0BH
A huge variety of silks for decorative awnings, cushions and loose covers.

Malabar Cotton Co Ltd, 119 Altenburg Gardens, London SW11 1JQ
Colourful Indian checked, striped and plain cottons.

Melin Tregwynt, Tregwynt Mill, Castlemorris, Haverfordwest, Pembrokeshire SA62 5UX
Wool throws and blankets.

Pukka Palace, 174 Tower Bridge Road, London SE1 3LR
Checked, plain and striped cottons.

Sanderson, 112–20 Brompton Road, London SW3 1JJ
Striped and checked cottons and linens in good blues and natural cream shades.

Muriel Short Designs, Unit 2 Hewitts Estate, Elmbridge Road, Cranleigh, Surrey GU6 8LW
Lots of muslin and linen in bright colours.

Fencing, trellis and gates

Buckingham Nursery, 57 Tingewick Road, Buckingham MK18 4AE
Beech, hazel, holly and lavender hedging.

Clifton Nurseries, 5a Clifton Villas, London W9 2PH
Simple wooden trellis.

English Hurdle, Curload, Stoke St Gregory, Taunton, Somerset TA3 6JD
Willow hurdle fencing.

New England Gardens, 22 Middle Street, Ashcott, Somerset TA7 9QB
Picket fencing.

W H Newson & Son, 61–79 Norwood High Street, London SE27 9JS
Chestnut and plank fencing and sheds.

Weald & Downland Open-air Museum, Singleton, Chichester, West Sussex PO18 0EU
Wattle hurdle, woven hazel fencing and besom brooms.

Florists

Decorate your table outside with cut flowers, herbs, pots of lavender, or bulbs like amaryllis from the following:

The Flower Van, Michelin House, 81 Fulham Road, London SW3 6RD

McQueens, 126 St John Street, London EC1V 4JS

Paula Pryke Flowers, 20 Penton Street, London N1 9PJ

Wild at Heart Flowers, 222 Westbourne Grove, London W11 2RH

Food

Carluccio's, 28a Neal Street, Covent Garden, London WC2H 9PS
Wonderful Italian breads, pasta, cheese, oils and fresh wild mushrooms.

Steve Hatt, 88–90 Essex Road, London N1 8LU
The best fresh fish and shellfish.

Monmouth Coffee House, 27 Monmouth Street, London WC2H 9DD
Really good coffees.

Neals Yard Dairy, 17 Shorts Gardens, London WC2H 9AT
Excellent British cheeses.

Planet Organic, 42 Westbourne Grove, London W2 5SH
Organic goodies such as wheat grass.

Spitalfields Organic Market, Commercial Street, London E1.
Every Sunday. Bread, fruits and vegetables sold from a collection of stalls in the old fruit and vegetable market. The best is Wayside Organics from Sussex, who sell really fresh salad all year and, in season, old-fashioned apple varieties, tomatoes, runner beans, courgettes and pumpkins.

Furniture and accessories

Aero, 96 Westbourne Grove, London W2 5RT
Modern furniture, including metal cafe chairs and tables, simple china, glass and bright plastic accessories.

Blacks Camping Shop, 53–4 Rathbone Place, London W1P 1AB
Kettles, tin mugs and Swiss army knives.

Chalwyn Ltd, St Clements Road, Poole, Dorset BH12 4PF
Traditional metal hurricane lamps.

The Conran Shop, Michelin House, 81 Fulham Road, London SW3 6RD
Lots of outdoor living ideas, such as lanterns, galvanized metal buckets, terracotta flowerpots, wooden plant labels, gardening hats, tools, folding cricket chairs, garden tables and hammocks.

Designers Guild, 267–71 & 277 King's Road, London SW3 5EN
Great ideas for coloured table linen in fabulous combinations of pink and orange, or bright lime green, in checks and florals; plus a good range of simple bowls and jugs for stylish tables, and brightly coloured cushions, tableware and baskets.

Habitat, 196 Tottenham Court Road, London W1P 9LD
Seasonal garden furniture including folding tables and chairs, lanterns and flowerpots, plus a range of brightly coloured PVC fabric for tablecloths.

Cath Kidston, 8 Clarendon Cross, London W11 4AP
Retro 1950s-style junk furniture that is updated with a lick of paint. Also look out for zinc-topped kitchen tables which would look equally good outside.

Muji, 26 Great Marlborough Street, London W1V 1HL
Lightweight folding canvas and metal director's chairs, plus paper plates and cups, and metal lunch boxes that are practical for picnics.

Paperchase, 213 Tottenham Court Road, London W1P 9AF
Good selection of paper napkins, paper cups and paper by the roll to make practical disposable tablecloths.

Price's Patent Candle Co Ltd, 110 York Road, London SW11 3RU
Huge selection of candles.

V V Rouleaux, 10 Symons Street, London SW3 2TJ
Ribbons in all widths, textures and colours for edging cushions or for making ties.

The Source, 10 Harbour Parade, West Quay, Southampton SO15 1BA
Shopping shed with cheap home accessories and lots of ideas for outside tables.

Garden designers and specialists

Lisa Bynon, PO Box 897, Sag Harbor, NY 11963, USA

Timothy Leese, Holkham Nursery Gardens, Holkham Park, Wells-Next-the-Sea, Norfolk NR23 1AB

John Matheson, 4 Tredegar Terrace, London E3 5AH

Nancy McCabe, Nancy McCabe Garden Design, Inc, PO Box 447, Salisbury, CT 06068, USA

Dean Riddle, PO Box 294, Phoenicia, NY 12464, USA

Garden supplies

Banks Horticultural Products, Angel Court, Dairy Yard, High Street, Market Harborough, Leicestershire LE16 7NL
Will deliver top soils, 1 to 25 tonnes, in the Midlands only.

Fair Field Turf, Fairfield Court, Brookland, Romney Marsh, Kent TN29 9RX
Range of soils and turf delivered nationally.

Muck Composts by Post, Lady Muck, Marswood House, Whitegate, Forton, Chard, Somerset TA20 4HL
Organic manure on 48-hour delivery.

The Organic Gardening Catalogue, The River Dene Estate, Molesey Road, Hersham, Surrey KT12 4RG
Organic garden supplies delivered nationally; a good range of fertilizers, including seed and potting compost, seaweed meal and Chase organic fertilizer.

Outside eating

Barbeques, picnic kit, simple white china, durable glassware, practical plastic, and cotton and plastic table linens.

BhS, 252–8 Oxford Street, London W1N 9DD

B'zar Spitalfields Market, Brushfield Street, London E1

The Conran Shop, Michelin House, 81 Fulham Road, London SW3 6RD

Debenhams, 344 Oxford Street, London W1A 1DF

The Dining Room Shop, 62–4 White Hart Lane, London SW13 0PZ

Divertimenti, 45–7 Wigmore Street, London W1H 9LE

Graham and Green, 4–7 Elgin Crescent, London W11 2JA

Habitat, 196 Tottenham Court Road, London W1P 9LD

IKEA, 2 Drury Way, North Circular Road, London NW10 0TH

Jerry's Home Store, 163–7 Fulham Road, London SW3 6SN

Peter Jones, Sloane Square, London, SW1W 8EL

John Lewis, Oxford Street, London W1A 1EX

Liberty, 214–20 Regent Street, London W1R 6AH

David Mellor, 4 Sloane Square, London SW1W 8EE

The Pier, 200 Tottenham Court Road, London W1P 9LA

Summerill and Bishop, 100 Portland Road, London W11 4LN

Young & D, Beckhaven House, 9 Gilbert Road, London SE11 5AA (trade supplier) Retail outlet: Belle du Jour, 13 Flask Walk, London NW3 1HJ
Traditional Greek barbeques.

Woolworth's Plc, Head Office, Woolworth House, 242–6 Marylebone Road, London NW1 6JL

Paints

J W Bollom & Co, 15 Theobalds Road, London WC1X 8SL
Extensive range of colours.

Brats, 281 King's Road, London SW3 5EW
Mediterranean water-based emulsion paint with a chalky texture, in vibrant colours.

Cole & Son Ltd, 142–4 Offord Road, London N1 1NS
Small range of period paint colours, including a good terracotta shade for courtyard walls and flowerpots.

Crown-Berger, Crown House, PO Box 37, Hollins Road, Darwen, Lancashire EB3 0BG
Wide range of colours and exterior finishes.

Dulux Advice Centre, ICI Paints, Wexham Road, Slough SL2 5DF
Huge range of colours and textures for exteriors.

Farrow & Ball Ltd, 33 Uddens Trading Estate, Wimborne, Dorset BH21 7NL
National Trust colours in a range of

period shades; Cooking Apple Green looks good on trellis and furniture.

Marston & Langinger, 192 Ebury Street, London SW1W 8UP
Good sludgy garden colours, in finishes especially designed for outside use.

Benjamin Moore & Co, Montvale, New Jersey, NY 07645, USA
Good range of period colours.

John Oliver, 33 Pembridge Road, London W11 3HG
Small range of excellent colours, including verdigris, as great shade for garden furniture, pots and trellis.

Sanderson, 112–20 Brompton Road, London SW3 1JJ
Wide range of paint colours.

Plants and seeds

Chelsea Gardener, 125 Sydney Street, London SW3 6NR
Extensive array of plants, pots and garden furniture.

Clifton Nurseries, 5a Clifton Villas, London W9 2PH
Everything for a well-furnished garden: clematis, honeysuckle, cactii, topiary box, herbs, bedding plants, plus a huge range of flowerpots and trellis.

Columbia Road Flower Market, London E2 (Bethnal Green tube)
Held every Sunday morning – a great source of cheap bulbs, cuts flowers and plants in season.

Croftway Nursery, B2233 Yapton Road, Barnham, Bognor Regis, West Sussex PO22 0BH
Specializes in bearded irises in yellow, white, orange, mahogany and pink, hardy geraniums and other perennials.

Deacons Nursery, Godshill, Isle of Wight, PO38 3HW
Late-summer dessert apples, cider apples, quinces, walnuts, blackberries, cherries, figs, plums, peach trees and many others available. They have a list of vines suitable for the British climate, and a good selection for the wine enthusiast.

Future Foods, PO Box 1564, Wedmore, Somerset BS28 4PW

All sorts of unusual vegetables and edible plants from seed and tubers: asparagus, pea, cucumber, courgette, hairy melon, lemon basil, rice, rocket, sea kale, and lily white and wood blewit mushrooms.

Grooms, Pecks Drove Nurseries, Clay Lake, Spalding, Lincolnshire PE12 6BJ
Bulbs for autumn and spring planting.

Halls Nursery, West Heddon Nursery Centre, Heddon-on-the-wall, Newcastle upon Tyne NE15 OJS
Dahlia specialist.

Hexham Herbs, Chesters Walled Garden, Chollerford, Hexham, Northumberland NE46 4BQ
Herb specialist.

E W King & Co Ltd, Monks Farm, Kelvedon, Colchester, Essex CO5 9PG
Flowers and vegetables, including 100 sweet pea and 40 lettuce varieties.

Langley Boxwood Nursery, Rake, Nr Liss, Hampshire GU33 7JL
They specialize in *Buxus*, commonly known as boxwood, and make wonderful hedges and topiary for pots.

Old English Roses, David Austin Roses, Albrighton, Wolverhampton WV7 3HB
Climbing roses and modern bush roses – 900 varieties, some rare.

The Organic Gardening Catalogue, Chase Organics, Coombelands House, Surrey KT15 1HY
An extensive range of products selected for the organic enthusiast: Jerusalem artichoke, dwarf French beans, cabbage, carrots, leeks, sea kale and strawberry seeds – all available by post.

Parkers Dutch Bulbs, 452 Chester Road, Old Trafford, Manchester M16 9HL
Specialize in tulips.

Provenance Plants, 1 Guessens Walk, Welwyn Garden City, Hertfordshire AL8 6QS
Seasonal deliveries of plants by mail order, including foxgloves, lavender and auriculas.

Reads Nursery, Hales Hall, Loddon, Norfolk NR14 6QW
The largest range of fig plants for sale in Britain – they also supply asparagus, sweet oranges, lavender, wisteria and plumbago.

Roses du Temps Passe, Woodlands House, Stretton, Nr Stafford ST19 9LG
A wonderful collection of old roses.

Sandeman Seeds, The Croft, Sutton, Pulborough, West Sussex RH20 1PL
Seeds of rare plants.

Scotts Nurseries, Merriott, Somerset TA16 5PL
Apple trees have been a speciality of this nursery for more than a century; they also have figs, nuts, walnuts and rhubarb, plus climbing roses, old-fashioned roses, violas, delphiniums, peonies, and clematis.

Simpson's Seeds, 27 Meadowbrook Road, Old Oxted, Surrey RH8 9LT
Basil, broad beans, 'Gardener's Delight' red cherry tomatoes, big green beefsteak and standard red 'Amateur' tomatoes. Plastic solar domes to protect seedlings.

Thompson & Morgan, Poplar Lane, Ipswich, Suffolk IP8 3BU
Seed specialists, including vegetables and blooms such as sunflowers.

Van Turbergen UK, Dept 836, Bressingham, Diss, Norfolk IP22 2AB
Bulb specialist.

Second-hand shops and markets

After Noah, 121 Upper Street, London N1 1QP
Factory and school-house-style junk furniture, including simple wooden chairs, and shoe lockers and old-fashioned meat safes, which are useful for unusual garden or shed storage.

Alfie's Antiques Market, 13–25 Church Street, London NW8 8DT
Everything from 1960s furniture, to old fabrics, second-hand chairs, tables, china and glass.

Bermondsey Market, Bermondsey Square, London SE1 (London Bridge tube). Every Friday morning.

D A Binder, 101 Holloway Road, London N7 8LT
Factory and old office furniture.

Brick Lane Market, Brick Lane, London E1 (Liverpool Street tube). Every Sunday morning.

Castle Gibson, 106a Upper Street, London N1 1QN
Factory tables and chairs for robust outside dining ideas.

Decorative Living, 55 New King's Road, London SW6 4SE
Good for old metal folding cricket chairs, garden benches and tables.

Portobello Road Market, Portobello Road/ Westbourne Grove, London W11 (Notting Hill Gate tube). Every Saturday.

Bryony Thomasson, 19 Ackmar Road, London SW6 4UP
Antique French ticking fabrics (by appointment only).

Tobias and the Angel, 68 White Hart Lane, London SW13 0PZ
Old pots and gardening tools, plus metal watering cans, and junk tables and chairs.

Sheds and greenhouses

Country Garden Buildings, The Garden Studio, 42 Crossway, Harpenden, Hertfordshire AL5 4QU
A variety of classic garden sheds and summerhouses.

Greenhouses Direct, PO Box 290, Royston, Hertfordshire SG8 6UA
Huge range of greenhouses.

Homebase, Beddington House, Wallington, Surrey FN6 0HB
Wide range of simple garden sheds.

Tools and accessories

A1 Laboratory Supplies, 2a–4 Avery Hill Road, London SE9 2BD
Bell jars to protect delicate seedlings.

Action Handling, The Maltings Industrial Estate, Station Road, Sawbridgeworth, Hertfordshire CM21 9JY
Utilitarian metal mesh storage ideas for sheds and outhouses.

Alitag Plant Labels, Unit 10, 131 Bourne Lane, Much Hadam, Hertfordshire SG10 6ER
Aluminium labels with metal punch writing and pencil labels for plant names.

Aston-Matthews Ltd, 141–7a Essex Road, London N1 2SN

Everything for kitchens and bathrooms, plus shower fittings and taps suitable for outside use.

Avant Garden, 77 Ledbury Road, London W11 2AG
Wonderfully exotic utensils such as hand-made pitchforks from Andalusia, Spain, antique tools, terrracotta pots, gardener's string and decorative garden furniture.

The English Garden Collection, PO Box 1030, Radley, Abingdon, Oxfordshire OX14 3SA
Every garden accessory from watering cans and children's tools, to ornaments, furniture and flowers.

Garden Trading Company, The Old Brewery, Priory Lane, Burford, Oxfordshire OX18 4SG
A wide range of gardening tools.

General Trading Company, 144 Sloane Street, London SW1X 9BL
Garden accessories.

Graham and Green, 7 Elgin Crescent, London W11 2JA
Contemporary lightweight folding aluminium deck chairs and sun-loungers, plus fold-up slatted cricket chairs and tables in a variety of colours.

Haemmerlin Ltd, The Washington Centre, Halesowen Road, Netherton, West Midlands DY2 9RE
Galvanized wheelbarrows.

Hawes Watering Cans, 120 Beakes Road, Smethwick, West Midlands B67 5AB
A good selection of old-fashioned metal watering cans.

The Heveningham Collection, Weston Down, Weston Colley, Micheldever, Winchester, Hampshire SO21 3AQ
Hand-crafted iron furniture for interior and exterior use, from chaise longues, dining tables and chairs to Versailles tubs.

Hortus Ornamenti, 23 Cleveland Road, Chichester, West Sussex PO19 2HF
Handmade traditional garden tools.

Jerry's Home Store, 163–7 Fulham Road, London SW3 6SN
Deck chairs, folding chairs, picnic kit, glass storm lanterns and metal hurricane lamps.

Windrush Mill Garden Catalogue, Station Lane, Witney, Oxfordshire OX8 6BH
Foldaway wheelbarrows and terracotta long tom pots.

Underfoot

Civil Engineering Developments, 728 London Road, West Thurrock, Grays, Essex RM20 3LU
Green marble pebbles, Scottish beach pebbles and beige granite setts.

Dorset Reclamation, Cow Drove, Bere Regis, Wareham, Dorset BH20 7JZ
Flagstones, paving bricks and quarry tiles.

Fired Earth, Twyford Mill, Oxford Road, Adderbury, Oxfordshire OX17 3HP
Import Spanish terracotta tiles,

Adrian Hall, The Garden Centre, Feltham Hill Road, Feltham, Middlesex TW13 7NA
Old red-brick Tudor tiles and Victorian paving setts.

The Kasbah, 8 Southampton Street, London WC2E 7HA
Red and blue glazed Moroccan terracotta tiles.

Leisuredeck Ltd, 311 Marsh Road, Leagrave, Luton LU3 2RZ
Timber decking.

Ribble Reclamation, The Brick House, Ducie Place, off New Hall Lane, Preston PR1 4UJ
York flagstones, cobbles and reclaimed architectural items.

J & J Shellfish, Alexandra Dock, Kings Lynn, Norfolk PE30 2ET
Cockle shells to make a path.

Solopark, The Old Railway Station, Station Road, Nr Pampisford, Cambridgeshire CB2 4HB
Reclaimed building materials plus old red-brick pavers for paths and courtyards.

Jane Cumberbatch's best-value suppliers

Top-ten UK suppliers

Z Butt Textiles Ltd, 24 Brick Lane, London E1 6RF
Denim, silk, calico, fabulous white cotton drill and muslin (all cheaper per metre if you buy at least 10 metres).

G J Chapman, 10 Penton Street, London N1 9PF
Hardware shop with a good range of pea sticks, flowerpots, compost and other garden supplies.

Habitat, 196 Tottenham Court Road, London W1P 9LD
Colourful cotton by the metre, folding tables and chairs, deck chairs, umbrellas and stacks of good-value tableware.

Homebase, Beddington House, Wallington, Surrey FN6 OHB (with branches around the country)
Pots, sheds, practical metal bins, kitchen-ware, storage boxes, giant green recycled plastic bags for transporting garden debris, plus a good range of plants like foxgloves, delphinums and spring bulbs.

IKEA, 2 Dury Way, North Circular Road, London NW10 0TH.
Basic wooden tables and chairs, white folding cricket chairs, cheap glass tumblers and boxed sets of plain white china.

John Lewis, Oxford Street, London W1A 1EX
Hardware department for garden tools and accessories, plus fabric, wool blankets, and cushion and bolster pads all sizes.

Ian Mankin, 109 Regents Park Road, London NW1 8UR
Great for cotton checks and stripes for cushions, awnings and covers, it always has some on sale at great discounts.

Russell & Chapple, 23 Monmouth Street, London WC2H 9DE
Canvas, cotton and linen.

Staines Catering Equipment, 15–19 Brewer Street, London W1R 3FL
White catering china (mugs, plates and bowls) – good value and sturdy for outside use.

Woolworth's Plc, Head Office, Woolworth House, 242–6 Marylebone Road, London NW1 6JL
Good for basic garden kit, kitchenware and bright plastic picnicware (branches around the country).

Top-ten foreign suppliers

Ruby Beets Antiques, 1703 Montauk Highway, Bridgehampton, NY 11932, USA
Painted furniture, old white china, kitchen-ware, including battered old food nets, simple pressed-glass jugs and enamelware.

The Conran Shop, 117 rue du Bac, 75007 Paris, France
Deck chairs, flowerpots, smart metal tables and other garden accessories, as in its English counterpart.

El Corte Ingles, Calle Hermosilla 112, Madrid 28009, Spain
Department store with everything from outdoor furniture to simple tableware and food (branches around the country).

Crate & Barrel, PO Box 9059, Wheeling, IL 60090-9059, USA (mail order)
Crate & Barrel, 650 Madison Avenue, New York, NY 10022, USA (shop)
A wonderful source of good-value furniture and accessories, from simple china and glass to table linens.

Finca El Moro, Fuenteheridos, Huelva 21292, Spain
A guest house for walking, riding and alfresco eating.

IKEA, 101 Rue Pereire, F 78105, St Germain-en-les-Laye, France
For home basics at great prices, including folding cricket chairs, lightweight fold-up tables and cheap, stylish kitchenware.

Catherine Memmi, 32–4 Rue Saint Sulpice, 75006 Paris, France
Crisp cotton and linen table linens.

Smith & Hawken, 2 Arbor Lane, PO Box 6900, Florence, KY 41022, USA
Great range of garden tools, plants and accessories (stores across the country).

Christian Tortu at Takashimaya, 693 Fifth Avenue, New York, NY 10012, USA
The American counterpart of the French specialist – a heavenly florist with cut flowers, topiary trees and scented candles.

Vert Vous, 91 Boulevard Raspail, 75006 Paris, France
Supplies of everything you could possibly need for the garden, from straw hats and hammocks to next season's bulbs.

Acknowledgements

It has been enormous fun putting together *Pure Style Outside*. It would not have been possible without all the hard work and support from everyone at Ryland Peters and Small. Special thanks go to Jacqui Small, Anne Ryland, David Peters, Penny Stock, Zia Mattocks and Janet Cato.

Fiona Craig-McFeely and Alice Douglas have been superb assistants. Thanks also to Clair Wayman, Jen Gilman (our wonderfully versatile nanny), Lynda Kay and Robert Davies for his expert help in Spain.

Together with energy, humour and enthusiasm, photographer Pia Tryde has produced beautiful and descriptive images. I must also thank Nick Pope and Ian Skelton for the splendid cut-out photography.

Many thanks also to the following people who have so kindly let me photograph in their gardens: John and Colleen Matheson; The Manor Gardening Society; Nancy McCabe; Dean Riddle; David and Carolyn Fuest; Humphrey and Isabelle Bowden; Nick and Hermione Tudor; Vanessa de Lisle; Karl and Pia Sandeman; Lisa Bynon and Mona Nehrenberg; Timothy Leese and Robert Chance. Special thanks to my New York friend, Tricia Foley, for her help, guidance and hospitality, and to Ellen O'Neill, who very generously let me invade her Long Island home once more.

Big hugs for Alastair, Tom, Georgia, Grace and my parents, John and Jean, who, once again, put up with me and the agonies and angst of creating a book.

Index